Reactions, Reviews

This book is a hugely important addition to the canon of literature on grief. It is a searing, uncompromising and deeply personal account of grief both as a raw experience and from the point of view of someone who has a comprehensive psychological insight. As a universal human experience, this book on grief is relevant to anyone but a must-read for those experiencing grief personally or working professionally in the field.

Katherine Cox *Psychotherapist*

In "All Things," Steve Barlow has created that most generous of gifts: both a way of helping himself through the time following the death of his brother, Stewart; and setting down his experience in a way that will surely help others grieving to muddle through somehow…What I really love about Steve's book is the liveliness and vigour of his writing. I think this vigour comes from the authenticity of his expression and the bitter-sweet hilarity that is a true aspect of life and death with those we love. Perhaps paradoxically, this is a movingly funny book.

Amanda Bettison *Counsellor*

Rarely have I been so touched by such raw, truthful and courageous writing. I am in awe of the author's ability (maybe because I am a therapist too?) to go so deep so fast and unapologetically let the reader have insight into his grieving process. By his generosity of truthful self-disclosure, his lostness and his rage and his confusion he offers the reader something unusual in this field: permission. Permission to have the courage to have their own journey through what they are experiencing, to 'find meaning in the madness', the messy business that is grieving.

Linde Raisbeck *Psychotherapist (Retired)*

The author is a friend and I know him as a proud, passionate man with a wonderfully volatile sense of humour. His lust for life is full of fierce tenderness, and he is a deep thinker. Just the guy to take you on a trip to hell and back, and then some. So brace yourself. His book is much, much more than a grief journal. The honesty of his writing will take your breath away. His wit will revive you, often with a slap in the face. And as a profoundly grieving man who is also a highly experienced therapist, his urgent and perceptive use of the extensive literature on loss and grief is like no other. As a reader I'm left full of admiration and gratitude.

Jim Holloway *Counsellor, Supervisor & Author*

Stephen has written a powerful piece after the sudden loss of a much-loved younger brother. It is an articulate and honest account of the exhausting physicality of the grieving process.

Christianne Heal *Psychotherapist*

Absolutely gripping. It is a no-holds-barred account of a personal journey and the accompanying references to the grief reading on sibling loss that thread through it, show a depth of exploration of the pain of grief that is rarely recorded. His writing is fluent and inspired and takes us into his dark places without ever being sensational or mawkish.

Revd Phil Sharkey *Hospital Chaplain*

I feel as if every sinew of my heart and soul have been stretched to breaking point …my soul is exhausted but couldn't stop or look away.

Phil Joslin *Jungian Analyst*

All Things

An adapted grief journal by Stephen J. Barlow

Dedicated to the bereaved, the bereft and the grief-stricken.

We are legion.

With love, profound thanks and deep appreciation to everyone who walked by my side during the dark night. I can't have been easy.

A Letter from the Author

Grief has its own full-force ferocity. It's the dark night of the soul, the deafening scream, hell on earth and like being hit by a truck. The metaphors go on and on and in time, you will conjure up and create your own. And for any of us who have experienced grief, up close and personal, they can barely come close to accurately describing or communicating to others what it is to endure life in the company of grief and loss. In fact, we could hardly be blamed for doing just about anything in our mere mortal powers to avoid keeping such company at all cost. But, as Shakespeare once wrote, 'there's the rub', the flaw in the plan. As mere mortals all, grief is, with few exceptions, the unavoidable, the undodgeable bullet. Why? Because we are all time-limited and to know that we ourselves will die at some point is to acknowledge too that we will also bear witness to the death of others, those we love, cherish and hold dear.

In my role as a therapist, I have over nearly twenty years, worked with many bereaved clients, battered by the storms of loss, who come seeking some kind of refuge from the relentless pummelling, albeit for a brief moment. Therapists are invited to take up a privileged position and bear witness as part of this often agonising, profoundly intimate reality. And as a client, I know how crucial it is to find someone willing to step into that very storminess, willing to journey alongside the anguish and devastation of the bereaved.

The 'being with' element of this is, I believe, the ground upon which all other possibilities can then be built. Because when the death of a loved one falls upon us from a great height, there is nothing but shock and awe as far as the soul can see and we can feel horribly alone. When we lose those who matter to us, grief feels like it's all we know. We are our grief and there seems little room for anything else.

But therapeutic support cannot be all there is as we negotiate a path through the wilderness of loss. Also, I did not feel inclined to write my journal from an explicitly therapeutic viewpoint (though to imagine my experience as both client and counsellor would not influence is a nonsense) and it is not intended now as some professional, intellectual pontification by any means. I wrote it because, in the midst of my own grief and loss, I felt some weird, uncharacteristic urge to see my words appear before me, in the hope that they might give some shape or form to this battle royal erupting on the inside. Stranded in the fog of it all, I craved catharsis, a distraction or even a momentary breathing space, which could provide something other than the relentless, voracious grief eating me up in the wake of the sudden death of my younger brother, Stewart. In other words, I made room for something else. These breathing spaces are not a cure, but they can offer ballast to ground us when the earth beneath our feet disappears and our pain feels without compare. This is the stuff of mourning and bereaved, we fall through time and space with little to hold on to.

And so my journal became my breathing space and I made my choice to occupy it as little or as often as I felt the need, write whatever came to mind and channel any and every part of me that emerged from the shadows or popped up unexpectedly along the way. I did not restrict myself by implementing any singular style, so the colour and texture of my writings ended up all over the place, sometimes sounding like a novel and at other times, a collection of loosely connected thoughts and feelings. But as unformed and freestyle as it seemed, it gave me a new awareness; I was still my grief but found too that I was so much more besides.

So why have I decided to 'go public' with my own record, a collection of scattered writings that cover exactly a year in the life of a death and the subsequent heart and soul-shattering loss that arrived in its wake? Well, I remember attending a conference on the psychology of addiction some years ago and was struck by a presentation made by a clinical psychologist, Martin Weegmann, on the subject of Alcoholics Anonymous and other 12 step fellowships. He remarked how he believed the power of storytelling was one of the most critical and effective elements of recovery, healing and transformation, strongly suggesting that the sharing of our narrative with others creates a unique, even vital sense of community and belonging. I agree with him although I also believe this power extends to all dimensions of what it is to be human and not an influence restricted to the realm of addiction. Author Joan Didion, who I reference extensively throughout my journal for reasons that will become apparent, wrote *'We tell ourselves stories in order to live'*, the idea being then that we may not actually survive if we did not or we would certainly be less-than. That may be over-egging things to a degree but since the days of cave etchings and wall carvings, maybe it is just something we feel compelled quite naturally to do. Maybe it lurks in our DNA. Indeed, how would we know anything if it were not for the telling of stories?

So, this journal recounts the first wave in the story of my grief, chapter and verse. When my brother died suddenly, science could not help me, facts offered little comfort and ill-conceived notions of charting progress via stages or steps had little impact. I also had no known blood family left to turn to. But then, out of the blue, I started to write. And I also became what I then termed a 'bereavement bore', buying text after tome after tale as I searched for, well, just about anything that might offer company and comfort. I found it in the shape and form of daily Amazon deliveries that ultimately ended up requiring their very own bookcase. While I read many wonderful books (I include a full reading list herewith), there was something missing in all the literary options - the raw, in-the-moment, uncensored ramblings of someone, anyone, that had been committed to paper as and when they were stranded in the grief blast zone, and then published. I had discovered *Mourning Diary* by the French philosopher, Roland Barthes, and as extraordinary as this testimonial is, I still craved something else, something more.

Here then, is my version of that 'something else'. And this is my hope; that my story, presented here as something of an experimental writing project, might provide to some, moments of fellowship, a breathing space and relief when you find yourself hit by the wave or quaking in the aftershocks of your loss. For sure, grief is an ever-changing, shape-shifting thing and I feel it would be remiss of me to leave the current covid 19 pandemic unacknowledged when at this time and on a worldwide scale, the global grief and loss playbooks are being agonisingly rewritten. But I do not come to educate, make promises, speak of healing and/or recovery or tell you everything will be alright. Because, as you already know, everything is ***not*** alright.

However, despite all of this and for what it might be worth, here it is, an episode from my very own tale of grief and loss, now committed to the firmament, where it takes its place in vast and expansive company, a starry dot of light in a universe of human stories.

Stephen J. Barlow June 2020

The Rules

So, these were just a few rules/conditions I imposed on myself as I prepared the writings for publication:

To censor or not to censor: I have read the journal many times since writing the final entry and unsurprisingly this stirs myriad emotions. I have laughed, cried and even been moved by much of my testimonial, well-versed though I am, but I have also cringed and winced as I don't always come across as the most reasonable or even likable individual. Grief can do that to a person. My narcissistic self would sooner cut and edit. Rest assured; I have resisted. However, while I'm perfectly entitled to expose myself, warts and all, I have made the executive choice to initialise certain figures for the sake of decorum. But these episodes remain otherwise intact. They also carry considerable weight in relation to our grief because when some figures that we hope will be there for us, simply are not, then it either compounds the loss or adds additional devastating layers to it. Other names may have been changed for legal reasons or simply because, when offered the option, some chose another moniker to be known by, a wish I fully respected. Also, one word has been redacted in the good name of propriety, so I shall leave that to your imagination.

What does 'an adapted journal' actually mean? Changes to grammar/structure: I have my favourite phrases/words (you will probably recognise them) but how many times does anyone want to read 'devastating', 'precious', 'volcanic' or 'awful' in one book (and sometimes in consecutive entries)?!? As a result, alternatives were found so you won't need to keep asking yourself 'haven't I just read this page?'

Changed/corrected punctuation is allowed. I want the journal to be comprehensible. Grief is crazy enough as it is without feeling like your brain and eyes have been assaulted as a result of reading about it.

Remove journal entries that seem to replicate in their entirety themes, experiences and perspectives covered elsewhere. As a result, seven entries have been eschewed.

Quotes: Quotes that head each journal entry have been added retrospectively and attempt to comment thematically on the journal entry in question.

Once upon a time…

I was a child of the 50's by all of four months, born into a middle-class family in the Midlands in August 1959, the middle of three brothers. We lived in a detached house in the village of Wychbold, a small parish just eight miles from the city of Worcester. We appeared happy, content and functional and as youngsters, for a time we surely were. But children don't remain children for long and I remember feeling too different from an early age to wear the mask of inauthenticity effectively, and my first attempts at 'coming out' as gay (while not actually knowing at the time that this was what I was doing) were met with parental hostility and a prescription for anti-depressants at the age of twelve. My younger brother also came to identify as gay but, observing from the side-lines and learning from the denial, shaming and homophobia with which my coming out was met, remained safe in silence until he was an adult.

But moving above and beyond the ties that bind, I went out into the world, professionally turning my hand to many things over the years. I've been a waiter (who hasn't?), a dance teacher, a massage therapist, a drag queen, West End performer, choreographer and therapist. My roles covered a veritable rainbow-coloured career spectrum and I remember them all. And I also remember the day in 1964 my younger brother was born, where I was, the time of day and the crisp, frosty and golden Winter weather that frames the memory. I recall the phone ringing and I have a distinct memory of answering it. The voice at the other end told me that I had a baby brother. Then, in April of 2017, fifty-two years and three months later, another call came through.

We bereaved are not alone. We belong to the largest company in all the world
-the company of those who have known suffering.

Helen Keller

Gone

Not all of our days were sweetness and light. Not all of our challenges were met in tender loving support. Through the years we drifted apart and returned over and over to the place siblings know - the knowing of each other, the knowing of ourselves, the knowing of the indescribable state of just knowing

Benjamin Scott Allen *in Grief Diaries: Surviving the Loss of a Sibling*

April the 6th 2017

It was just a day. There was sun. I saw some clients. I drank coffee. I pottered now and again, and I wrote up client notes. Yes, just a day; a predictable, comfortably unsurprising day. Then the phone rang. A woman's voice. I thought it was one of those call centre things.

'Hello. Is that Stephen Barlow?'

'Who is this?'

'My name is Hilary Harrold. I'm from The Weldmar Hospice. It's your brother, Stewart. He's collapsed'. A beat. 'It's serious'

I didn't know what any of this meant. I asked for details. Where was he? Nearest rail stations? What hospital?

'I'm on my way' I said and hung up. *He's collapsed…it's serious.*

So just go, I said to myself, go as fast as you can. Be with him. Comfort him.

Then, on this day to end all days - I have to see it written down visibly, tangibly, absolutely: Thursday the 6th of April 2017 – as I grabbed the essentials (wallet, rucksack, toothbrush, pants, socks and that's it), my mind threw together a plan, maybe a map, of how I was quite sure this ghastliness would all pan out. Just get there, I thought, and all will be well when all is said and done. All will be well.

And whatever desperate fantasy I needed to concoct in that moment was based on blinding flashes of something like film that spilled out of my short-circuiting brain. And it goes something like this...

I arrive at the hospital. I don't know what it looks like, so I just construct something generic, glued together from memories of a hundred movies, TV shows and my own limited experience. I hurry through a series of doors as if I know where I'm going. I look driven, terrified but driven. I know where I need to be. At my brother's side.

Back to now and my reality, and, as my fantasy continues to play out alongside adding texture and colour to the narrative, I multi-task, checking that taps are off, the windows closed, electrics unplugged.

Cut to fantasy: Ahead of me in the ICU, I see a figure, helpless, unconscious, vulnerable. My stomach twists and wants to throw something up. I know this recumbent body, barely moving, is Stewart. I can feel myself breathing weirdly and I can hear my heart beating in my ears as if it is actually in my ears. I see tubes, bags of fluid, machines going blip, lights maintaining a line and a leap motif to signal life. *Cut to...*

In the stillness, I sit next to him in his fragile, poorly state. I hold his hand and I tell him I will never leave him like this, never leave him to face this alone, never leave him as long as he's scared and needs me to stay. Because he is my brother and he is precious. Yes, I tell myself as I plan to leave my Hertford home, it is along those lines that this will play out. Life is about to change, and I will be there for Stewart, no matter what it takes. I will be there. Simple.

My mobile rings and shocks me back into my Thursday morning madness and mania. Another Dorset number. Don't answer it, something tells me. But I have to and I do.

'Is that Stephen Barlow?'. A man's voice.

'Yes', I say. My fantasy plan starts to crack.

'I'm phoning about your brother, Stewart...'. The cracks turn to rumbling sounds.

'I'm so sorry...'

Don't say it, don't say it, don't say it, don't say it, don't say it...

'I'm so sorry. We tried to revive him...'

And that's all I remember. I hear it still.

Tried to revive him, tried to revive him, revive, revive...we tried.

With a bang and a shudder, the fantasy is no more. Shattered, it lies at my feet. I don't think the doctor ever said the word dead. I don't think I let him because he knew I knew. And I do know that, at this nano-moment, something changed in me for all time as I lowered myself to the floor, holding my phone and mumbling feebly 'Oh my god, oh my god, oh my god. This is a nightmare, this is a fucking nightmare' And all the while the doctor simply says over and over 'I'm sorry, I'm so sorry'. And I think I was doing something akin to whimpering.

All I say thereafter is 'I'll be there' and I'm left in darkness, pain, disbelief, fear, panic, collapse and dread. But for all that, I know somewhere in me that I will get to my brother as soon as I can, and nothing will stop me. And he will be dead, but I will still hold his hand and kiss his cheek and I will still be there for him as long as he needs me to be and I will love him always.

The fantasy lies in ruins, burnt out, smoking and destroyed. It was not to be. My brother is dead.

The Chapel Part 1

Every loss changes us; you'll never be the person you were before your brother or sister died

T.J. Wray *Surviving the Death of a Sibling*

Friday the 7th of April 2017

The brother I love has died. The life I lived, over. The world I knew, ended. Grave new world.

I sit with Roger, my closest of companions, who yesterday dropped everything to journey with me, and I wait. For friends, for partners. For the two Steves.

Crumpled in a Costa in Dorchester South, just minutes from where Stewart's body lies still and cold in a Chapel of Rest, we while away minutes that feel like hours. No, that's not true. They feel like nothing, ticking by in nothingness, surrounded by an imitation of life, which to everyone else milling around us is simply 'life'. But to me it's the darkest, longest night of the soul where the time/space continuum just imploded, and the day is about one thing and one thing only - I have to be with my brother.

Little Steve and Stewart's partner Steve join us. We hug. We don't collapse to the ground wailing, all flailing limbs and grief-stricken purple faces. We hug and talk softly and silently scream with anguish and pain. And only we can hear it. We hear the scream of the other and that is intimate and terrible and bonding all at the same time.

I call the hospital. They are ready. Stewart is ready.

I share the news and within minutes we arrive, pre-occupied with the practicalities and directions until there we stand, not outside some Gothic portal with thunder murmuring in the distance but a nondescript wooden door in a nondescript hospital corridor, with walls slathered in moss green paint. Nurses, patients and admin staff pass quietly back and forth, the silence only broken by the occasional trolley or gurney.

Even at a time like this, etiquette and what is 'proper' bothers me, all of us, I think. None of us know whether we should press the bell. We maintain this oh-so-British position for a while. Then, I press the button, which immediately illuminates the tiny rim of light around it. The door opens. A young man stands there. He gestures for us to enter.

In a small, airless enclave with a curtained window to the left of me, we all sit in the L shaped configuration of chairs. The young man who is also called Stuart (three Steves and a Stuart/Stewart? Really?!) sits and waits as do we all. That's because we're not all here yet.

'We're just waiting for another brother' I say and almost immediately realise that I cannot bring myself to say *my brother*. Stuart just smiles as if to say 'that's fine'

We sit. It is so quiet. Little Steve begins to cry. And if memory serves, I did something really weird. I think I rubbed his foot or his ankle or something. It was right next to me, I remember, and I just wanted to make contact with him to let him know I was there. So, I stroked his foot.

I am being strangled by grief. My throat is in agony, my face burns like someone just put a match to it and my breath is gathering itself to explode into this tiny room with such unearthly power that the walls crack and the roof blows off. My tears simply do not know how to turn off and it's like losing control of my bodily functions. That's it then. This is where I die too, I think to myself. Then the bell sounds and as the door opens, I feel something like dread. It's the brother I have not seen for twenty-one years. The sight of him is almost frightening, certainly disturbing. I stand and we do this awkward hug thing and I feel he doesn't want to let go while I want to turn back time and un-hug him before I black out.

Next, we all sit, the energy in the room now almost tangibly changed. Then I speak.

The Chapel Part 2

I don't want to be left alone. I don't want to go on, brotherless. I don't know how. I might as well go on headless. He is my geography, my map. I need him

Elizabeth DeVita-Raeburn
The Empty Room: Understanding Sibling Loss

'What is he wearing?' I ask.

'A linen robe, like a gown…' replies Stuart.

A what!?! I think. Sounds awful.

'…and a silk purple blanket'

And I wish I hadn't asked.

'Are his hands covered?' I know where I'm going with this.

'Yes, covered'

I turn to the Steves. 'Which hand?'

They know what I mean.

'It's the left one. Yes, the left one' they tell me. They knew. I didn't. I turn to Stuart.

'Little stars' I say dreamily as I my touch my own hand 'My brother had these little star tattoos on his hand'. My throat constricts again, and I feel like I'm about to make some guttural noise as I see Stewart's tattoo constellation in my mind's eye, and it's an image that rips at and squeezes my heart. ' Are you allowed to uncover his hand?' I ask, though I'm barely audible.

'Yes, of course. The left hand?' he checks.

We nod. Stuart smiles in a polite, young man kind of a way and enters the chapel. Moments later he returns. No words. So I stand and I hope, and I pray, and I slowly walk into the chapel.

Closing the door behind me, I turn my head slightly toward the bedecked platform to the left and there, just feet away, lies my brother. In the second that it takes to process what I'm experiencing, all that comes to mind is '*Will I survive this?*' I don't mean metaphorically in any way at all. I stood there, I looked at my brother's dead body and I believed that there

15

was a chance, a possibility that I would not survive.

I walked around the side and gently took his hand. So, so cold.

'Stewie, you're so cold' I remember saying 'You're so cold'

And I kept repeating it over and over and over

So cold, so cold, so cold, so cold. On and on and on as I stroked his skin.

And I just kept caressing his pale, boney hand, whiter than white and colder than marble in winter. And my tears rained down on to his little star tattoos, which I had always thought were so very odd and at the same time so very Stewart. And I rubbed my tears into his skin because I wanted to leave him with a bit of me, somehow, in some way. So I left him my tears. Because they belonged to him.

None of the old clichés really resonated for me when I looked at Stewart's face. He never looked his age. That gentle, boyish face never did and never would look fifty-two. It was bright and alive. Not now.

What cliché could comfort me, I wondered? *Cliché 1* – He just looks asleep. Well, he doesn't. *Cliché 2* – He's not really there anymore. Yes, he is because I'm looking at his unhappy and distorted face and it's killing me. *Cliché 3* – It was a good death. Enough.

It's agony, it's ugly, I'm dying by the second, I never want to leave him and I am fucking furious with anguish and rage and red-hot pain and I just want him back and it's wrong and unfair and there is no God and if there is one then he's a **** and I hate him. I really fucking hate him.

Collapse.

Silence.

Restore.

I know I have to go so I tell Stewart how much I love him. I stroke his hair and another grief monster grabs me in the gut. But I still gently stroke his hair and talk to him, almost as if I feel I have the power to offer some comfort even now. There are tubes still protruding out of his nose and his mouth from the unsuccessful attempts to revive him and I wonder why there is discolouration like a bruise on his left temple. Did that happen when he fell, I wonder? I'll never know. But I do know this is the deepest, darkest, scariest place I have ever been.

'Bye Stewart. Bye my brother' I say, my face now distorted also and puffed up and far, far, far away from any kind of peace. And with that I walk wretched and destroyed from the room, knowing that if I do not leave now, it is likely I never will.

Home

*I seemed to have crossed one of those legendary rivers that divided the
living from the dead, entered a place in which I could be seen only by
those who were themselves recently bereaved*

Joan Didion *The Year of Magical Thinking*

The 8th of April 2017

As I opened the door, my senses came alive and I drowned in my brother.
Memories and flashes pinned themselves to my brain, turning it into a
memorial wall inside my skull.

I stood in the hallway of Stewart's flat, comprising a long windowless
hall, lounge/kitchen to the left and bedroom at the far end. And there
was that smell. Oh, my goodness, that smell was overwhelming; scented
candles, Issy Miyake, coffee, something not quite eliminated from the
previous owner and Stewart. How do I describe the Stewart smell? Well,
it's like a clean-ness and something a bit old fashioned, maybe a touch of
beeswax and something gentle and reassuring too.

I walk from room to room, drinking it in, every bit of his essence. It's
a home that could only belong to my brother. There are surprises at every
corner, little nests of knick-knacks, retro bric-a-brac and fairy lights draped
from every bookcase and window rail, strung through the bed headboard
and draped around Tallulah, Stewart's mannequin companion, muse and
co-star of many a show and cabaret. What on earth will she do now? Poor
Tallulah. She will never be loved like this again.

As I enter the bedroom, another evocative scent hits me. I realise it's
emanating from the dressing gown right next to me, hanging from the
door. I put my arms around it, barely registering what I'm doing, and I

sort of slump into it. I hug it tenderly and push my face into the towelling material, deep, deep into the fleecy fabric and I cry and cry and cry. And in between I inbreathe the comfort it offers, almost like some junkie getting a fix. And like an addict, I cannot imagine how I will live without this. It is as if it symbolises life itself, this baggy, comfy robe. But Stewart's not in it. He is here and at the same time, never will be again.

The two Steves are with me and do the things I simply cannot bear to do. They clear kitchen cabinets, check everything is switched off, empty the fridge and pack up the food. I am touched by the attention they pay things, their deep affection for Stewart and their extraordinary kindness towards me. They don't have to do this, but they want to do this. I just know they want to be here with me, even though they don't know me. Without them, I would by now have gone quite simply mad.

'I'll wash these few things if you like' offers little Steve from the kitchen.

I turn to him and see the last kitchen bits and bobs my brother will have used on the morning of the day he died; a plate with some crumbs of toast, a mug sporting rings of coffee residue and a cafetière, still half full.

I say 'Let me' gently and I move to the sink.

I take my time. The last breakfast, I think to myself. I rinse the cafetière very slowly almost not wanting to empty the contents, feeling as if I'm disturbing some sacred site. Am I defiling it, I wonder? I keep washing gently, as if I am washing my dead brother, the way they do in some religious rituals to this day. I'm not religious but I get it. I perform the act with tenderness and care and love and then it's done.

Finding comfort in each other, we sit and talk, pausing every now and then to be in our own world, space and memories of Stewart. The swirling, endless sadness swims around the room like it's some big aquarium of grief. We simply get lost in ourselves, snapping back into the moment only when blazing afternoon sun slides into the room illuminating a shelf of richly coloured glass pharmacy bottles arranged in a line on the bookcase.

For now, there is nothing else I can do. It's time to leave Bournemouth. This time last week, Stewie - I and few others called him Stew or Stewie - and I were speaking on the phone, laughing, bitching, camping and talking about Bette Midler's return to the New York stage in *Hello Dolly!*

'So how was Bette?!' he had asked excitedly.

'Just amazing and not in her usual way' I shared with equal enthusiasm.

'She is sooo Dolly!' he replied

'Soooooooooo Dolly!!' I agreed 'You should have been there. Why didn't you come??' I whined 'It just wasn't the same without you'.

And that is my truth, Stewart. It's just not the same without you.

Ritual Part 1

Only people who are capable of loving strongly can also suffer great sorrow, but this same necessity of loving serves to counteract their grief and heals them.

Leo Tolstoy

The 5th of May 2017

The Hallmark Hotel in Bournemouth is perched perilously on the very edge of the cliff on a strip called East Overcliff Drive, offering spectacular, almost otherworldly views across the English Channel with the French city of Cherbourg in its 'as the crow flies' eye line, but farther away than any human eye can see. Today, however, for me, the incandescent vista barely registered. I sensed things but that was all. There was no Cherbourg, France to consider or any other place in the world for that matter. I could barely experience the hotel as a real place if I'm honest, so I certainly had no picture of the planet beyond. My world was about my brother, past and present and the rituals of the day, creating them, hosting them and maybe somehow surviving them. There was nothing but deep breathing, a heart beating faster and faster – was I too about to endure sudden, unexpected cardiac arrest? - and achey pain in my throat, face and neck as I either resisted the crying or committed to it. Either way, it hurt like nothing else. Because today was the day. Today was the day I buried my brother.

It is an irony that at a time when you want to drag yourself into the darkest corner of space, there is an expectation that you will need to function at a higher level than you would under any other circumstance. And so, I would do my best for Stewart, for his friends and for myself but, with no dress rehearsal, all bets were off.

I remember standing on the balcony of the hotel lounge, staring out over the sea as the sun, so bright this awful morning, rolled out a gold carpet across the water that ended at the edge of the vast and impressive stretch of beach. This shoreline, gorgeous and sandy and not at all like that ugly, gravelly thing in Brighton just down the coast, also lit up with the morning. But all I felt was barely contained anguish, confused as to why I was here looking at this dazzling early Friday morning weather picture in the first place. No other guests were up. It was just Jenna, the two Steves, Viv, another of Stewart's nearest and dearest, and myself, standing, sitting and then standing again in the empty lounge, half-heartedly sipping at coffee while we awaited the arrival of the funeral car that would take us to the crematorium in Poole.

Don't come, I prayed, *don't come and then it won't be true.*

If you find yourself at times like these blessed enough to be surrounded by the right people – and I had been so blessed – it would seem there is an unspoken contract forged between you all. Tuning in to one another, we spoke in whispers sometimes, then silence, then more whispers and a passing holding of hands, tears shed in forlorn recognition and then more silence, sometimes a warm, desperate embrace and then an acquiescence to the inevitable. For us all, gathered there in the face of this unspeakable, shocking loss, it was a quiet thing that morning.

Almost with a respectful acknowledgement that this area had, just for a fleeting moment in time, become a sacred space, the hotel receptionist almost *sotto voce*, informed us that the car had arrived. *So, this must be real then*, I thought. And we stepped out into the sun and began the journey.

I sat with Jenna, my salvation, my rock, my dearest of friends, who had, without hesitation arranged to be here with me, despite having two small adorable children reluctant to let her go anywhere without their written permission. So, we sat looking forward, her arm through mine and the highly polished white seashell box resting upon her lap which contained a hundred or so rose petals. I had prepared them earlier that morning, gently plucking each one from the stem with painstaking care and diligence. I cannot ever remember performing any ritual with this much deliberation and I doubt that I will again.

With little to stall or slow our journey, we arrived at the crematorium with time to spare. As we turned into a driveway, a winding path surrounded by verdant foliage with sun everywhere, I closed my wet eyes. And then I opened them and the first person I saw, walking it would appear aimlessly and lost, was the other brother. I said nothing but looked at Jenna. 'Is that Richard?' she asked. I told her it was. She simply held my arm a little firmer.

As the car pulled up to the main entrance, there was a distinct possibility that I was simply going to become so inconsolable at the sight of the coffin containing the body of my brother, that I would collapse or have a seizure. And that would be it. *Sorry, folks, show's over. Nothing to see here. You can all go home.* And all the while, I'm spirited away on a gurney, never to be seen again. But in a mere moment, everything changed for me, because then, as people I had never met before arrived looking shocked, bereft, devastated and overcome, I felt a sense of them and the love they held for Stewart and their own catastrophic loss and grief. Friends spanning four generations from those in their twenties to those in their eighties, from his workplace, from the theatre company he performed with right through to old friends from Brighton to the men and women in his life today.

Over one hundred people turned up at the service that day to say goodbye to Stewart. My fantasy that this would be a mere handful of nearest and dearest and the cremation service would be a ghastly formality to somehow simply endure, collapsed under the weight of the truth. And I knew that I could do this, and I would, for want of a less grandiose word, triumph. Because as numbers grew, this extraordinary entourage provided me with the vital missing ingredient without even knowing it. Suddenly, as more and more arrived, this event that I was so desperate to avoid, became undeniably meaningful.

'I think we should begin' the funeral director whispered to me, as the coffin was gently repositioned to commence its journey down the aisle of the little chapel. *Can't we just freeze this moment in time*, I thought? But what I said was...nothing. I took a moment to see Stewart in front of me, the men at his side to help him on his way, Jenna to my left and then finally, I took in the congregation to either side of us all, sitting, waiting, not knowing. And, informed as I am by my showbiz roots, that was my cue. So I just nodded. Richard, the funeral director, moved slightly forward and gestured to the left of the chapel and, as he did so, the ritual began.

First, came the music. That oh-so-familiar piano chord softly played over and over before those classic vocals began, vocals that have such history for Stewart and I and that evoke magic and now mourning in equal measure. Slowly, down the aisle we proceeded as The Divine Miss M, Bette Midler provided our soundtrack. I zoned in and out but remember something about love and rivers and bleeding souls. Rather, I went inside myself, to find myself, to prepare myself and to hope for the best. And then, reaching the last, front pew, Jenna and I waited as Bette sang her closing refrain and Stewart took his place in the bright light at my side.

Then, that moment. The song ended. *Ready or not*, I thought again, *that is my cue.*

And so, armed with my words, printed out and placed in a specially bound presentation book, I took a first step as Jenna moved silently to the side, taking a place next to Viv, just a breath away from the raised platform where I would soon be standing. Behind me, I heard the congregation sitting and settling. *Keep going.* I walked slowly but with purpose to the lectern. *Too late to worry now*, a voice tells me. *You're on.*

The brother I love is now dead and lying in a wooden box next to me, a simple spray of brightly coloured spring flowers bedecking the top. I had been very clear about the flowers. Two months ago, Stewart and I were laughing, debating, enjoying and discussing, quite at ease in each other's company and watching the movie, *La La Land*, wondering what all the fuss was about. What the hell happened? Will someone please tell me?? No time to get lost in that now. I open the book and I look up. Quiet.

And so, I open my mouth to speak, wondering if anything will come out. It does.

Stewart Barlow - Cremation Service 9.30am 5 May 2017

Reflections (full text)

Let me be honest with you all. For a time, I contemplated every possible option that could offer to me an escape from all that was to transpire on this dreaded day, let me off the hook if you will, a get-out clause that would allow me to just sit feeling wretched and huddled and exhausted and anguished. And while I do feel those things, I do not feel only those things. But still, it is the 'cop-out' I seriously considered in my darkest, most desperate moments over this past month. 'Hire a humanist, a celebrant, hand it over to a priest' I thought. And then I spoke to a close friend, who, having suffered her own significant losses, shared with me her process. 'Consider one word that best describes how you want this day to be' she said 'one word that captures in its essence how you want to shape the day and let that be your anchor' - and immediately I knew the word - authentic. I wanted today to feel authentic. Because that is who and what Stewart was. So, inspired by my friend's suggestion, the die was cast and I believe it falls to me - or should I say us, for we will all play our part in some way - to make this truly sad and reflective day a very real testimonial and service to a very genuine and dear person to us all.

I love my brother very much. I am devastated and my heart is broken. I miss him and the cruel reality of that loss bludgeons me awake each and every day at the moment. I think we all probably look for something to comfort us at times like this, knowing as we do that nothing really can. Our grief is a terrible, inevitable thing. It feels monstrous and yet it is not a monster. It simply, catastrophically is. However, while we might know that to be true, that is not enough to stop us looking everywhere, endlessly, as we seek solace. We search the heavens, we look inside ourselves, we turn to the love and care and unwavering presence of friends...and we read. We seek out the recorded words of those who have lost and wept and screamed and howled at the moon in the name of their own devastating losses. And, bearing this in mind, I went in search...

In Jandy Nelson's book, *The Sky is Everywhere*, the character, Lennie reflects on her grief, following the death of her sister and she writes:

My sister will die over and over again for the rest of my life. Grief is forever. It doesn't go away; it becomes a part of you, step for step, breath for breath. I will never stop grieving Bailey because I will never stop loving her. That's just how it is. Grief and love are conjoined, you don't get one without the other. All I can do is love her, and love the world, emulate her by living with daring and spirit and joy.

Grief and love - you don't get one without the other. And that has stuck with me which is why I share it with you today. If the pain and anguish I feel now, is in direct proportion to the love and specialness of my relationship with my brother, then So.Be.It. And elsewhere in this quote, she could eerily be writing about Stewart. He was alive with his own 'daring and spirit and joy'. It may not have been ever thus. Our early years could be dark and tumultuous times and as children, while I recall some fleeting moments in time, we remained ghosts to one another. We traversed an often unpredictable path through those early years in our own ways and those paths rarely crossed but Stewart was to blossom, to grow and to become one of the most compassionate, loving and genuine people I have ever known and as adults we became truly, deeply significant souls in each other's lives - in other words, we found one another.

Don't misunderstand me, he was a flawed mortal like the rest of us. I have too much love and respect for him to recall him in chunks of selective memory. He could be tenacious, grandiose, icy, frustrating and if you said something that he found unacceptable, you got ... the look. And if any of you have ever got 'the look', then you don't forget it in a hurry! And you know something, I would not have changed him for the world. Because, fabulous flaws included, these combined to form the Stewart we all know and love and miss so deeply at this time.

Stewart never did anything in half measure. He was a teacher, a therapist, a singer, a partner, a friend, a tri-linguist, a musician *and he could even knit. And for the past nearly twenty years, he had been a committed and passionate counsellor, dedicating himself to a professional path that gave great spiritual meaning and purpose to his life and I truly believe to those he worked with. No half-arsed involvement but full-throttle commitment to anything he took on. And that list is only a 'taster' of all that he could do and everything that he was. And he really was the very definition of 'authentic', a friend who was true, dedicated and fearlessly loyal.*

And one of the major driving forces that we both had in our lives was the performing arts. We both loved theatre, musicals, drag, singing, dancing (Stewart not so much) and the divine Miss M herself, Bette Midler, whose spectacular tours took us from London to New York to Vegas in order than we could quite literally 'experience the Divine'.

Yes, Stewart really was an unstoppable creative muse, a driven artistic spirit. His artwork carried his own quirky stamp and contained a joyous, wide-eyed innocence that was easily recognized. If I had some of it here and held it up for all to see, you would know in an instant that this was, in its own way, a little piece of Stewart. And he played the piano and wrote music and stories and plays and he acted with passion and commitment and integrity, and of course the occasional sling-back and sequinned gown. He cared about the craft and his fellow actors and the text and accurately representing the thoughts and feelings and motivations of his characters. And most of all, he entered into the local world of performing art because he loved the people he started to meet and wanted to be part of that community, that family. And from the messages and acknowledgements I have received that have both touched and broken my heart, this love was a very profoundly mutual thing.

I will end there and hope to see you later at the Woodlands Burial Site where I know special friends will also want to share their own thoughts, feelings and reflections. On closing and as you slowly make your way outside, I would invite any of you to take a rose petal from the bowl, place it upon the coffin and spend your own personal moment with Stewart before you leave. This final piece of music was very special to Stewart. Thank you.

And I close the book. The music begins and I step from the lectern, white shell box in hand and I wait. No-one moves and for a moment, I wonder if there is some cremation etiquette that has frozen everyone in their seats. But then, little Steve, partner Steve, Viv and Jenna slowly stand and begin to move forward. I breathe again.

During the weeks that led up to this day, it was drawn to my attention that Stewart, in his hospice role as bereavement lead, had chanced upon a certain piece of music in the line of his work. It was Arvo Pärt's *Spiegel im Spiegel* and on hearing this composition, simple yet exquisitely beautiful, he had commented to a colleague that when his 'time' came, he wanted it played at his funeral.

An anticipation of death? I had wondered at the time - was this music that he had heard while helping a patient plan his or her funeral? It would have been the kind of thing that Stewart was tasked to do all the time and I can well imagine the support and compassion that my brother was able to offer to the dying at such times. Little could they have known then that, in this case, the choice of music would serve as inspiration for Stewart's own funeral that was to take place probably before their own.

One by one, each person stepped forward, silently collected a petal and then moved towards the coffin. I was barely sane at this point, so it pleased me to see myself simply in the role of petal monitor. But what this extraordinarily simple gesture provided was an opportunity for everyone – and remember, most were strangers to me – to connect with me fleetingly, just by receiving a petal. And then they had their moment with Stewart, their own precious and unforgettable final moment in time. For most, that split second with me took the form of eye contact, a glance full of mournful craving. Others gently placed their hand upon my arm or shoulder as they moved along. But for some, it was too much. Head bowed, they took the petal and disappeared quickly from my eye line. I understood. You look into my eyes; you look into Stewart's eyes. For many, the similarities offered comfort, for others, it was simply overwhelming and awful.

And then everyone had left, leaving just myself, Stewart and Richard, the funeral director in attendance. I had not looked at the coffin once while this part of the service played out but now, I did as I moved to place my own petal. I remember being taken aback at how oddly beautiful it was. Adorned with pinks, whites and deep reds, the lid of the coffin looked resplendent. Maybe us flawed mortals have just created all these creative, often lavish interludes as distractions, activities to take our mind off the truth of the day; that we walk with death, ours and others', always.

Pinks, whites and deep reds. It's very Stewart.

But I know my brother well and this really was very him. Again, I thought of the work he did on a daily basis and I have no doubt that he will have discussed this very rite with clients and patients as they worked together to create a funeral that was both meaningful and true.

Meaningful and true. Yes, that would have been my brother's wish and I hoped I had served him well on this day of days. I looked towards Richard, standing guard at the door. He smiled a gentle smile, you know, the kind that just acknowledges something silently. I looked back towards the coffin. The music continued to play, and my tears now just flowed, occasionally wiped away by a handful of tissues so as not to drench my suit. It's macabre maybe and yet not uncommon apparently but all I then wished to do, standing beside my brother for the last time, was to remove he coffin lid, hug him and kiss him 'goodnight'. Well, I couldn't hug him for obvious reasons so what to do? I hesitated but for a moment, before I stepped forward, bent slightly and gently placed my lips against the lid of the coffin. 'Bye, Stewie. I love you' I whispered.

I did not loiter thereafter. I stood back, looked around the chapel one last time and mopping up the mess on my face, walked slowly out into the sunlight, knowing that come the afternoon, I would have to do it all again.

Ritual: Part 2

It's human to create meaningful ritual…we create rites of passage to connect our worldly and our sacred life, to move us from where we are to where we must go.

Elaine Mansfield, *Author of Leaning into Love*
(from her TedX Talk 'Good Grief! What I Learned from Loss)

The Woodlands Burial Grounds…

Same day, different faces. But not all. The other brother is still lurking around. That's how I experienced him, lurking. Anyway, I avoid him to the best of my ability, as I prepare myself for this second ritual - the placing of Stewart's ashes into the ground in a shady, unspoilt dell set deep in the Woodlands burial grounds. It was a location that I had chosen one Friday some two weeks previously at a time now predominantly a blur. The other brother's presence - a wisp of something vague, a mere irritation at worst - does little to distract me from my quest, even though he keeps popping up like a spook and asking for a copy of the death certificate to present to his doctor.

Voices are hushed and speak in whispers until collectively it all sounds like white noise. Everyone is drinking tea or coffee and eating pastries. There are Danish pastries on one table and my brother's ashes on another and that is just too absurd to upset me. I am just taking it all in. The room fills up. Some people I know - Jenna, the Steves, Viv, the brother and a few returning faces from the morning - but most I have yet to meet.

And so, I begin again…

Reflections 2 (Full Text)

*Hello everyone. My name is Steve Barlow and I am proud to say
that I am Stewart's brother. Some of us have already met and many of
us meet for the first time today on this very sad occasion, following that
news some four weeks ago that I know has left us almost indescribably
shocked at the suddenness of Stewart's death. I know from the many
messages and acknowledgements, that we have all been devastated by
the loss of someone so dear to and treasured by so many - friends, a
partner, his work colleagues and myself. In the shadow of this, we all
take our own journey but today those paths converge here to remember,
to mourn and to mark this moment in time.*

*While I may have been left reeling, I knew that decisions and plans
needed to be made in order that we might all be here today. There was
no doubt in my mind that this service and all that it represents should
happen down here near the coast, where Stewart had chosen to make
his home, where he forged special friendships and where he chose to
work, to live and to flourish. I want this for him, and I also want this
for you. You were his family too.*

*At this morning's service, I spoke at length so this afternoon I shall
be brief. I know that others near and dear to him have moments to
share and I am so moved and touched that they do. Steve, would you
like to say a few words…*

I look towards my brother's partner, Steve and I also feel relief that I
can, for a moment, step aside. But as Steve begins to speak, he wavers, and
I fear he will not make it to the end of his 'share'. I take a small movement
towards him. I just want him to sense me there, in case he needs me to
step in. He doesn't. A moment later, he silently steps back into the crowd.
I breathe. And I continue.

*I am finding out so much about my brother from his friends and
I am grateful to have the opportunity to spend time with you. One of
Stewart's most treasured stories, I have come to learn, was The Little
Prince, a love he shared with one of his closest friends, another Steve,
who is going to read a passage from the story now…*

And the parade of Steves continues. 'Little' Steve (this is how he is so named in the land of many Steves, he tells me) steps behind the lectern and reads. He is confident and sure and focussed and there is no need for me to take a step toward him or indeed fear that I might need to. So, I'll just have to distract myself with something else that might need my attention at any given moment. With the reading complete, I watch Steve return to the gathering but not before I have, during the course of his presentation, discretely looked around all the faces in the room. There, crumpled, bent over, hunch-backed even, I see the other brother upon the sofa. He looks all collapsed in on himself, dead in a way. He stares during the reading, not towards Steve but at the floor. *You look frightful*, I think.

> *We will shortly move out to the Woodlands where Stewart's ashes will be placed. First, let us stand in quiet reflection as we listen to one of Stewart's solo recordings, taken from a studio album he made some years ago, when living in Brighton.*

I cue the music, which Richard, the funeral director, is set to play. He misses the introduction. *Shit.* He starts it over. Success. Together, in the lull, we all listen to *Dreamcatcher*, a song that Stewart apparently wrote. His partner tells me this afterwards. I feel bad that I did not know. Hearing my brother's voice today is understandably too much for some.

When the song ends, the lull lingers on, so I simply and slowly leave the reception room to begin the walk to the hole in the ground. Reconvened in the woodland glade, I continue…

> *When Richard very kindly showed me around the Woodlands, I knew in my soul that this was the spot, this unspoilt and wild enclave seemed somehow spontaneous, and just right for Stewart. So it is here that his ashes will be laid to rest and, indeed, it is also the spot that I have arranged for my ashes to be placed when the time comes.*
>
> *I would like to invite Stewart's friends Andy and Viv to share some very special words with you now.*

Both Viv and Andy look very far away, and I struggle to hear them but that doesn't matter. It's not for me. It's for them and others. What I do sense at that time however is a change in the weather and the sun and blue of the morning has now become blusterier and more overcast. *How appropriate.* It is now time to place Stewart's ashes in the ground. So this is it then, I think.

Richard, if you would.

And the funeral director steps forward next to the freshly dug pile of earth and the box is lowered. For a moment I think '*It's not very deep. How on earth will I fit in there too?!*' but that question drifts away quickly and I read Maya Angelou's *When Great Trees Fall*. By now, I'm reaching the end of my rope, having been running on empty for about six hours. Tightening throat aside, I get through it. *Gasp, breathe, relief.* And then, for the second time today…

Before we return to the reception area, I would invite any of you who so wish to take a rose petal from the shell box, place it on the casket and spend a moment. I am so moved that you all came today and that you were part of Stewart's life…

I gently remove the lid of the petal box. No one moves…AGAIN. Awkward. Seconds pass. Feels like minutes. Then, taking the lead, Jenna steps forward and that's all it took. In a kind of slow motion, everyone steps towards me, takes a single petal, spends a moment and then returns to the reception area at the front of the grounds. I am frozen, not in a traumatized sense but simply because I don't have the energy to move. Maybe I'll just fall in the hole too, I consider for a moment but there is only enough space for the immolated version of me so that's not an option. I'm miles away when the other brother suddenly appears at my left side, takes a petal and speaks. 'Well, mum was always wanting her boys to be together again, but I bet she didn't think it would be like this'.

And then he drops the petal on to the casket. Fortunately, he does not wait for any response from me and simply lumbers back to the reception. A relief for me because I just couldn't connect with those words in any way. So they sort of hung in the air for the briefest moment, floating and twirling before tumbling to the ground. Other than that, I could think of nothing I would want to say in return. Clearly, twenty years of resentment, befuddlement and estrangement is for me still alive and kicking.

But the day is coming to a close. I'm done in. Within an hour, everyone has left, other than Jenna, the Steves, Viv, Andy, Ginnie, one of my brother's oldest friends and a female friend of Stewart's from Brighton, who was unknown to me. We all deflate. We all hug a lot. We say very little. I thank our funeral co-ordinator, Richard and he says, 'It's been my pleasure to look after you'. I imagine he may say that to all the bereaved, but I pretend it's just for me and only today.

One last time, I look around.
And then it's over.

Celebration

I can accept the idea of my own demise, but I am unable to accept the death of anyone else.

Maya Angelou *When I Think of Death*

The 3rd of June 2017

Today, in The Oceana Room at The Cumberland Hotel, I'm hosting the celebration of life. I'm exhausted. No words.

Freefall

For many the funeral represents the end while for others it marks the beginning of something eternal.

Lynda Cheldelin Fell & Christine Bastone
Grief Diaries: Surviving Loss of a Sibling

The 4th & 5th of June 2017

Something, yet again, once more, is over. And like everything lately, when I take my leave, when I say goodbye, it is like another death.

I dreaded the curtain coming down on the celebration event for my brother. A judder fluttered through my brain like a little explosion well in advance and had already signalled a warning, but I think I pretended not to hear. The one thing I feared more than the day beginning was the second it ended. That was it. Rituals complete. Lights up. All done. I had punctuated the end of the first chapter.

Sunday floated in space, suspended and amorphous. I was in between something. That's part of the grief trademark. You don't know where, what, when, why or how. It could be this and it could be that. But it comes with a guarantee. You will become its slave and when it is done with you, you will feel either mad, incapacitated, bloodied or all three.

At Bournemouth station, as I said goodbyes that day to the two Steves, Viv and Roger, each hug and every fond heart-felt word cut me deep and I was again carried along on a wave of fear, angst, loneliness and terror. Everything was coming to an end and everything felt like death. And of course, the body never runs out of tears, so I was again awash with loss and longing, my body shaking as if hooked up to the National Grid. It wasn't poetic. It wasn't clean. It wasn't finished business. It was complete and utter fucking living hell.

As Monday arrived as shapeless and without form as the one before, I woke in my flat in Royston and waited. Nothing. And I waited some more. I heard cars, then a pigeon on the window ledge. Again, nothing. Of course, panic makes no sound, certainly not one that has a word to go with it. But within seconds or even less, as the cords of my faithful parachute are slashed and severed, I enter free-fall. And I panic.

And again it's 'Stewart, where are you, where have you gone?!?' but this time it's more desperate and I feel hysterical and very, very alone. It leaves me flapping about with no support around me, just hurtling towards, well, what? Suddenly, I have no focus, I have no purpose. I have no sense of who I am without something to create, to construct, to conjure. What do you mean there's no more rituals?!? Can't I just create one? Maybe a sequel? No. It's over. You're done.

I am beside myself. It's like Stewart just died again. And again. And again. And again. So I just keep hitting walls again. And again. And again. And again.

All I can do is just wander around, weeping, talking, mumbling and clenching my teeth. I bring the side of my fists down again and again on the kitchen sideboard, pain and fury all whipped up together into a smoothie of anguish and desolation. Not so refined and dignified today, are we? This hot mess of a bereaved brother has officially lost the plot and now, 'backstage' as it were, another truth, a messy, chaotic, blubbering truth, is kicking in.

But, isn't that the point. This tumbling through time and space is inevitable after all the booking, juggling, writing, phoning, Facebooking, creating, preparing, calling, coordinating, directing, facilitating, hosting, prepping and performing.

I'm fighting against it, with it and away from it. And then, in a moment of calm, simply because for a single moment I run out of steam and breath, I hear Stewart in my heart, and he says one simple, wise word. *Surrender.*

So I do.

Dark

...but my heart and body are crying out, come back, come back...

C.S. Lewis *A Grief Observed*

14th of June 2017

I hear the ticking of the clock. It's Stewart's clock. It offers me no comfort. Not tonight. I'm alone and it's late. Tick, Tick, Tick.

The thunder of disbelief rumbles in the distance. Damn, I didn't see that coming. Something in the heavy air nuts me in the face and as I disbelieve again for the millionth time, it roars a reminder that my brother really is dead. Ten weeks after that day and I still need to be shocked back into that reality at least once a day.

I listen to the clock and I look up. My mind goes all over the place, back in time, way back, picking up memories and images as it goes. Then zooming forward to that day, that ghastly, horrible day of death and shock and trauma.

It's the 14th of June but I'm back there. I hear a ringing phone. *Something something next of kin, something something collapsed. Pause. It's very serious.* The woman I came to know as Hilary tried to be calm, but I heard something frightful in her voice on that day.

So, I just lie there with all of this. And the clock ticks on. *Tick, Tick, Tick.*

Terrible Things

Tears are the silent language of grief.

Voltaire

15th of June 2017

Terrible things deserve our full attention. The images of the fiery furnace tower block tomb fill screens and front pages as shock and awe ripple red across this country and spread across the globe. The horror of Grenfell tower will never leave us. Nor should it.

Like the terror attack of the 3rd of June which coincided with my brother's Celebration of Life event at The Cumberland Hotel in Bournemouth, my reflections and feelings about this ferocious and shocking disaster I experience via my very own filter of loss and grief. Death comes with barely a whisper to many, a stealthy moment that rips life away with a dark, swift blade of fate. That was the death that took my brother while his back was turned, and within the blink of an eye and the beat of a heart, he was gone. For the living, it was a terrible thing. For him, well, we'll never know.

Then there is the death that comes in fiery leaps and bounds, leaving terror and trauma and screaming mouths and wide-stretched, tear-filled eyes in its wake. We just cannot imagine that, most of us. But for others, just a short journey from where I write this, this is the life they will know for all time, every pain-stacked second of every terrible day. Our hearts can break and break and then break some more. It is the only way. It is the only way if we are to remain human and not go insane.

These are the words I wrote on Facebook, the day terror swooped down upon the capital at London Bridge on the 3rd of June, while at the same time love filled a room some two hundred miles away in a hotel overlooking the sea.

The celebration of my beloved brother's life on Saturday showed me how much love, kindness, joy, care and compassion can be generated by a single life. And, as Saturday night unfolded with its horror, terror and destruction, I was shockingly reminded how the polar opposite is also devastatingly true. This is our world.

Some deaths are terrible things that in and over time, usher forth love, compassion, beauty, joy and fond remembrance. Other deaths, well, they are and will also be for all time terrible, terrible things.

Crazy

This was demented but so was I

Joan Didion *The Year of Magical Thinking*

The 16th of June 2017

Am I going mad? I feel like I'm going mad.

As the minutes, the hours, the days go by, I get ever-increasing moments of - oh, I don't know, what shall I call it? - depressurization maybe, release perhaps, transcendence even. That or I'm going mad.

In a Caffé Nero, I look at cake as if for the first time. *Cake* I think to myself as if I have just learned the word. I feel like Jodie Foster in the film *Nell*. Then, as I begin a session with a client, I think *'Is that **my** voice coming out of my mouth?'*. And I'm not Jodie anymore but instead I'm teleported into a Kubrick or Cronenberg nightmare, all disembodied and fucked-up.

Stewart Barlow, this is all your fault, I think to myself, aware that he probably already knows. Now my nights are filled with back pain and stomach upsets, probably some giddy somatic conversion, which results in plodding, lethargic days. But I keep working, feeling so very comfortable with the abused, the distraught, the bereaved and the addicted. It's like we speak a secret language without them ever having to explicitly know for a minute the relentless agony of my loss or to hear for a second the banshee wail that has been echoing around my soul for nearly ten terrible weeks.

I'm in the world but not in the world. I am not so much observing from inside a bubble - clients and therapists alike love 'the bubble' metaphor - as visited by flashbacks and snapshots of all that is going on around me while I observe from another plane, a parallel dimension. I'm aware but not, alive but barely. Yes, I'm really, really going mad.

So, as I prepare for the straitjacket, I drink coffee, wondering why I like it and remembering that Stewart absolutely, really, *really* loved his coffee (well, if the five bags we found in his flat just after he died are anything to go by). So, with Stewart in mind and heart and soul, I carry on drinking, comforted by the fact. Like I said, it's all a bit mad really.

This morning, I called Jenna and I tried to leave a message. After choking on a throatful of coffee – you remember, that stuff I'm having an existential crisis about? - I tried to speak and all the words kind of flipped, got jumbled and ended up just a noise. Then I had hysterics and thought it best to sign off before she played this disaster back and thought I was possessed. Elisabeth Kübler-Ross reminds us that there is a thin line between laughter and weeping where grief is concerned. Thanks for that, Liz because for a moment there I thought my grief, my loss, my swirling and spinning in a mess of bereavement really was a sign that I was going, quite simply, round the fucking bend.

Howling at the Moon

There is the feeling that you no longer want to live beyond tomorrow

Agnes Whitaker *All in The End Is Harvest*

The 21st of June 2017

Stages. Processes. Cycles. This model, that model...OK, stop right there.

I'm a therapist so I get why we need to see grief and loss and bereavement as a shape, maybe a graph, even a series of lines side by side, intersecting, paralleling etc. etc. ad infinitum blah blah blah. I use them myself, for heaven's sake. But the truth is, they offer but a thinly sketched picture of what it is to one moment be in free-fall, the next slammed into the black wall of anguish, then hurled into an abyss of pain that sends ripples juddering through your exhausted physical frame before you then might suddenly and disorientingly land in a kind of emotional flatline position before the whole ghastly thing starts over or turns into a brand new cycle of tumult. Like grief, that sentence was way, *way* too long.

Maybe one of the reasons for this touches on temporality. The you crying on your knees yesterday, dribbling like a baby and clawing at the floor is not the same you today going through what, to an onlooker, looks like the same regular come-day-go-day process of living the ordinary life. You're a day older, you've survived one more round of the sun and moon to get here, another twenty-four-hour period of simply not exploding in agony in the middle of the street. If nothing else, you at least know this. But that can only come with the passage of time.

And some do not survive. That's not in the stages anywhere. Some will head for the exit, opt-out, cast off the mortal coil or speed their own demise. I don't blame them. As the universe came tumbling down and trauma, shock and pain rained down, I wanted to die and did not care if I did. *Take me now*, I messaged to the powers-that-be. In fact, magically I thought, take me instead as if I were in a position to bargain with the gods. But then, an existential dilemma arose because then I would be exposing Stewart to **this**. I would be gone from the mortal plane as Stewart shook with terror and fear and dread. And that would be the point they made, those fuckers on Mount Olympus.

I struggle to find the same meaning and purpose in my world now. One moment, I can be sardonic and amusingly cynical about this whole white-hot grief thing while the next all I can do is sit zombified and stare at the inherited little deco vase on the sideboard. And the lavender coloured crystal, and the clock and the cat-shaped money box, black with pink stripes. These are Stewart's special things (I tell myself I'm just looking after them for him). *Help me*, I plead silently to this line-up of quirkiness, *help me to find my way, help take away my pain, please help my brother come back to life*. On and on and on.

So maybe frameworks, processes, stages and that whole kit and caboodle are really, really helpful because they give us an anchor, a little stability in an ocean, stirred by the convergence of savage storms, where deep, deep down in those watery depths perils and scary creatures lurk and prepare to pounce. You'll never know when they might emerge, but you'll know when they do. You'll never know how or if you'll survive but you can pray that you might. Thank goodness I've got those stages, graphs and diagrams to cling to in the meantime.

Beasts

...then comes a sudden jab of red-hot memory...

C.S. Lewis *A Grief Observed*

The 22nd of June 2017

Sad. Depressed. Stomach-ache. Back pain. Paranoid. Confused. Alone. Tired. Empty. Full. Upset. Head split. Throb. Manic. Unfocussed. Child. Scared. Alone. Sad. Sad. Sad.

Sad doesn't even come close to the feeling. It's a bit like describing World War 2 as a slight disagreement. Not even close. Imagine the biggest thing ever. Well, that is how deeply, deathly sad I feel. Groundhog Day sadness. Not oh-what-a-shame sad, not oh-if-only sad but I-actually-don't-know-if-I-can-endure-this sad. Sometimes I even bore myself with how sad I am. I get on my own nerves as I do the washing up and cry, cook food and cry, sit on the toilet (my location of choice currently) and cry. I might be knackered but I can always find the energy somewhere to cry, produce mucus, wail silently (you know, the body racking retching thing that happens when weeping REALLY gets its teeth stuck in) and convulse to an Olympic standard. It's ten weeks since the phone rang. To the day.

I see clients but I don't think I'm very good at what I do at the moment. I don't know how present I feel, how connected I am or what I can really offer. I keep expecting them to say 'Did someone die? No really. Did they? Because you're just, like, not here at all' because I fear my grief might as well be writ large all over my body, or like the scene in *The Exorcist*, when Father Karras visits the possessed, wheezing Regan as the words *Help me* manifest eerily upon her stomach. Help me.

But it goes round and around and around and it's 6.30 in the evening and here I am again and again and again. This time-machine trauma that whips me wickedly back and forth between past and present leaves me breathless. I'm so tired it feels like I'm throbbing. Do you know that feeling? It's like an achy heat thing that pulses away, flooding your extremities with a moaning psychosomatic wallop. It takes all those grief-riddled feelings feeds them through a blender and it comes out in the body with such a crash that you feel like a fever just hit.

Stewart, where are you, where are you, where are you??? Come back, come back, come back. Here we go again.

For some reason, that deep, dark descent into the valley of death in April is back for an encore this hot and stuffy but overcast eve in June. It's like a wall-engulfing tapestry of life and death memories, every room in my flat, an agonising arras of the shock and awe which somehow represents that journey to my brother and the days and nights of longing that came thereafter. I am grief.

How utterly awful this is. I mean really, utterly awful. I feel like screaming 'Oh no, not you again!' like it had gone somewhere. But it waits, like carnivorous beasts in those TV nature programmes that are spine-chilling, but you can't tear your eyes away. Big grief beasts that stalk and surround the injured, the vulnerable, the lame, each taking a turn to move in stealthily and then slash and bite and claw, leaving the poor creatures frozen in terror, never knowing when or from where the next attack will come.

Yes, that's how it feels today, ten weeks on. I'm surrounded. Come close. I won't struggle. Or resist. *Once more, surrender.*

To Die

But how did he experience it?.. The 'moment of terror', the 'eternal dark'?

Joan Didion *The Year of Magical Thinking*

The 24th of June 2017

Stewart, what's it like? What's it like to die?

I have wanted to ask that question every day since Stewart left me. Questions, questions, questions. Maybe I want to know if it hurt, if he cried, if he had a moment when he knew just before lights out that this was it, that thing we call death. But maybe I really want to know if he thought of me. I hope so. I hope he felt me with him, seeing him off, telling him I would be with him soon.

And maybe (I hope) he heard again those words that I had spoken to him in a small New York hotel in 2004, when he was emotionally unwell, scared, wrestling with psychosis, vulnerable and breaking down. That time when I said, taking his hand 'I love you very much and I will never let anyone hurt you'. He was an adult but always my little brother.

And you aren't here with me anymore, Stewart but I say it to you again nonetheless even though now it's kind of pointless and a bit late.

I love you very much and I will never let anyone hurt you. But this - the death thing - even I couldn't fend this one off.

Shit

"I lost my touchstone" she said "I lost the person who understood my family just as I did. I lost the mirror that was our face"

Jeanann

Elizabeth DeVita-Raeburn
The Empty Room: Understanding Sibling Loss

The 26th of June 2017

There is something so utterly shit about dealing with death when it comes dressed as business. Anyway, I'm back here again, sitting at a big oak table, with its matching chairs and its branded notepads and its matching pens and I understand that probate is about to begin.

'So, you cannot do the pledge here' says James the solicitor 'There's a solicitor waiting for you just down the road…'

I think: *What the hell IS going on. Are you messing with me?*

'You just need to go to her. Put your hand on the bible…'

Then I think: *I need to WHAT?!?*

'…and recite what she tells you. It won't take long. I said 10.30. It's only over the road'

Then: *And then what? Drink from the goblet of fire I suppose.*

But what I actually say is 'OK', like this is just a normal morning in Royston town.

'And I've spoken to your brother…'

And suddenly, I'm guarded.

'OK'. I'm full of eloquence and wit this morning.

'And with respect…'

Then I DON'T say: *Under no circumstances say my brother's name and the word 'respect' in the same sentence.*

But I do think it and I wish I could find the courage to say it.

'...it wasn't exactly clear in my first letter that I needed him to respond'

'OK'. I'm really excelling myself today.

'So, the death benefit will probably just get divided equally and... deal with you direct...form to sign...some kind of I.D...'

His voice kind of split into chunks and then faded like an audio effect and I suddenly didn't want to be here anymore with James blathering on and on while some trainee something or other sat there writing stuff looking about as engaged as a republican at a press conference.

And all I could hear was my estranged brother's name bouncing around and off the rafters of my brain until I thought my skull would crack.

When the estranged one arrived at the chapel of rest a hundred lifetimes and a billion tears ago, I distinctly remember thinking that it should be him – why wasn't it him? - lying on that slab, cold and alone. *Why isn't it you? why isn't it you? WHY ISN'T IT YOU?!?* In my head, I'm shouting this. I'm shouting this in his face and the words rip at his skin, leaving marks like burns.

I do not feel at all related or connected to my living brother and I am clearly more than willing to cast him as the villain of the piece, where he can become the target for the dark, vicious and rageful side of my grief.

In the wake of our mother's death in 1996, the three Barlow brothers kept company, brought together, as so many are, by the passing of a parent. A veneer was maintained, the estate was dissolved, and we mourned the loss of our mother in very different ways. But we did it together with a splendid and appropriate degree of courtesy and good manners. Stewart and I were close by this point in our lives, we had been through a lot and supported one another when crisis and storms hit...and boy, had we seen some bad weather! But for me, the eldest brought a dark energy to the place, something unspoken, unnerving. I knew from our early years, how enraged he could become and he, like our father, could be quick to anger.

By early Summer of 1996, our mother's ashes now interred at the same village church where she was married, and the family home emptied and sold, our work in the Midlands was done.

And at some point, the first born chose to cut ties. How it played out for Stewart I will never know but for me, he simply never turned up with his son for a planned visit. And for nearly ten years, silence. Then, he made brief contact with both Stewart and I as his marriage splattered onto the rocks and a court case loomed large. We did what we could. We offered advice, contacts, support group information, resources for counselling and spoke with him at length on the phone. Then it dawned. He wanted us to take him in. We both said no and felt duped. Silence.

Then, on the 6th of April 2017, when I entered the dark night, I had some mental aberration that quietly suggested to me that maybe this utterly unknown person, who had rejected both Stewart and myself some twenty years earlier had at least the right to know. I have said since that I believed that the decent and humane thing to do was to tell him. Ask nothing of him but tell him. And I still believe this to be true. But is it all?

In still moments, when I'm alone – and I'm alone often – I sense an unwelcome truth push through. It emerges from a place quite woeful and forlorn but emerge it sure does, and it hints at something unpalatable. In those first moments, maybe spanning an hour or so, just after I was told that Stewart had died, I think I needed something – anything – to hold on to that was somehow linked to the legacy of my family, that knew where we had come from and what that was like. No one else had been there to experience as children the rolling fields behind the house, the Summer days spent building dens out of hay bales, the snakes in the backyard, the Hardy gang that we feared and the spooky abandoned manor house, Amphlett Hall, a rambling old hall, straight out of Stephen King's *Salem's Lot*, that thrilled and chilled in equal measure. In that terrible moment, my estranged brother became something else - a symbol, a touchstone, a link to a past, a past that Stewart and I talked about always with joy, with sadness, with horror at times but always with a sense of a unique shared experience. Because we were both there. It was uniquely about our lives and our heritage. And that had gone in a single flash of tragedy.

On the 6th of April as I reached Kings Cross, I reacted with a knee-jerk desperation that came at me from a panic-stricken place and I made contact by speedily messaging one of his daughters, a name that for years had just gathered dust on my Facebook friends list (why did she 'friend' me all those years back? Teenagers friend EVERYONE, that's why). Within minutes, the brother I had not seen for 21 years was on the phone. I told him why I had messaged and almost immediately wished I hadn't. Too late now. His intention was to drive to Dorchester the next morning.

While I do believe that our sibling had every right to know about Stewart's death, this motivating factor was only part of the story. What happens when, grief-stricken and in shock, you realise with horror that you alone carry the history of a certain generation, at a certain time of a certain family? You make an excuse is what you do, and you call up a stranger, who you remember with fear and loathing but who at least knows about the fields and the hay bales and the snakes and the spooky old house.

And so call him I did.

Because there was no one else left to call.

Retreat

For these women, the sad recognition of their lost shared future with their sibling was as painful as their absence on a daily basis

Brenda J. Marshall *Sibling Loss Across the Lifespan*

The 29th of June 2017

So far it would seem, I *can* actually do the thing I most feared lost to me. I can, as it happens, be screaming in the valley of grief and still attend to my clients, all of them broken, bowed and bruised in their own way and we can be together, work together and they can feel safe. My non-disclosed but ever-present grief, my full-throttle anguish did not destroy them or freeze them in an icy block of terror. *So, Stephen, you can breathe, and you didn't lose your shit.* But let us not test the fates unduly and now it's time to stop and step back. It's time to walk the walk and know when to slow down, stop running and turn and face that thing behind you. I don't need to know how I just did what I did for the past several weeks and I no longer fear a return to my consulting room, my supervision role or the hospice (Yes. Imagine that. A hospice). I've passed the test. This one anyway.

But tonight, writing, reflecting and contemplating my navel, I imagine a knock on the door and before I can say 'relapse', that big-mouthed Grief gremlin thing towers above me again. 'Miss me?' it asks cruelly.

And it hurls up the inconvenient truth I have been frantically trying to dodge and, while I might duck and dive to avoid it with a certain dexterous aplomb, it gets me in the end, no matter how much ducking and diving, bobbing and weaving I do. Stewart is still dead. And part of me, I think a part I have held in blissful ignorance while I got on with the stuff of life, can see me write these very words and wonders even now why I would even pen such a thing. Surely, it's a lie. Surely it's just some mad, psychotic break you've had, it says to me, and you'll haul yourself out of that distorted reality and he will be there, calling up to catch up, sending a text to tell you he loves you or just Facebooking a response to some campy, dumb picture you posted because it made him laugh. *I'm afraid not, dear boy, he's gone.*

So, I'm taking my foot off the pedal, I'm slowing down, I'm daring to look up and out. Because it is time to stop. And oh my, what scary spectres you have held at bay so very well in days gone by. But here they come. Do I really - I mean really - want to take time away from the fast lane of the past three months if this is what I have in store? It's like a grief G-force wind tunnel that has the skin on your face flapping with fear, threatening to rip it clean off if you don't hold on tight. So you hold on tight like you've never held on before. Because now you know that you haven't been 'moving on' at all. You've been distracted and, with your back turned, *it* has been gathering speed.

I thought, really thought, that I had transitioned and that I had now passed through the *my brother has died and I don't believe it* place (where you feel like you're kind of gaslighting yourself) to the position of *He's gone. It's true.* But no, not today. And maybe I shouldn't be too surprised. It has been just eleven weeks to the day since I was whisked away by death and his cronies, grief, trauma, loss and shock. They still have me bound and gagged.

So now let's get on with this. I'm stepping down for two weeks. I'm officially closed for business. No clients, no rituals, no planning and nothing to offer sweet respite. This is the first time in the new place, armour off, naked, fully exposed. And I'm dreading it because straddling the divide between the land of the dead and the land of the living is terrifyingly unsustainable. Because you never quite know which one you might end up in.

Journey

Everyone can master a grief but he that has it.

William Shakespeare *Much Ado About Nothing*

The 30th of June 2017

What a grim yet perfect evening in Birmingham. Rainy, overcast, depressed. So comforting. But maybe I'm just being mawkish because sunny and blue would have been fine too. Actually, I couldn't care less what the weather is. I'm somewhere else right now where it's actually the nothing-ness of it all that is giving me the heebie jeebies – swirling, nebulous goo just all around me. Is this a grief thing? Oh God, I'm sick of all this detective work. Is this grief? Is that grief? Frankly, I know exactly what it is. It's fucking exhausting.

I am now officially a bereavement cliché. The books I'm devouring on an hourly basis speak of this inclination/compulsion, an obsessional drive to read all and anything that regales with tales of the grief-stricken. And here I am doing it daily. And I cannot speak for all the bereaved and grief stricken people in the world but I am scooping up everything I can find and building a raft out of it so I don't drown in this unforgiving ocean with all these relentless, yanking, tugging undercurrents. Dropping dead would be a relief compared to this but nah, that hasn't happened thus far.

So anyway, back to my raft. Well, I have welded together quite a vessel to date. C.S. Lewis, Virginia Ironside, Elizabeth Kubler Ross (of course) and my latest, Joan Didion. Joan and I took the train together earlier and what extraordinary company she turned out to be. When, as she begins to tell her story, she writes of her husband *'John was talking, then he wasn't'*, I knew I had chanced upon the right book. From what I understand, that was how it was for Stewart. I did not witness it. I feel deeply for those who did however, while envying them not one jot. He was here, then not. Alive, then not. Gone.

As Didion continues her astonishing narrative, my own memories, fantasies and fears get triggered one by one. As she writes of her husband's belongings handed to her by the hospital staff, I remember that green sealed bag still waiting to be opened in Stewart's flat. It contains the clothes he was wearing when he died. I dream that if I stare at it long enough, it might just start breathing. When she mentions the fall her husband John took when he collapsed and the bruise she saw on his face thereafter, I think of that reddish blue mark on Stewart's forehead. I remember wanting to put something on it, like witch hazel or some such because it looked like it must have hurt and in that moment in the chapel, I wanted to make it better. I guess he hit it on something as he fell. I hope he never felt anything.

And then there's the blood, the blood she cannot mop up so the cleaner attends to it the next day. And now I'm sitting here wondering, is there blood on Stewart's clothes like there was on Joan Didion's husband because there was blood on the tubes that protruded from his nose and mouth when I saw him in the chapel of rest. *Blood and bruises*. I cannot even begin to know what that means to me in this context. It's too much. When will it not be?

PART 2: Later that night…

As usual, I've been reading. Melanie Klein believed mourning was quite literally an illness. Bollocks. Stupid cow.

Joan

The truth is none of us knows what happens when people die

Virginia Ironside *You'll Get Over It: The Rage of Bereavement*

The 1st of July 2017

Death is my life. Everything is now, no longer life lived with Stewart on planet earth, but life lived without Stewart on planet earth. That is a crystal-clear and irrefutable truth which renders my life and everything in it different for that one simple (simple inasmuch as it is a cold, hard fact) bottom line.

I slept badly, due in part to a stuffy hotel room with a broken fan but also because I had eaten late, and my colon has always been something of a stress mirror. Of late, it has been mirroring consistently and uncomfortably and last night was no exception. But I drifted off as sun rose and did not then wake until 9.30.

So, I am wandering around the city and stopping every hour or so to spend yet more time in the company of Ms. Didion, my steadfast companion on this trip of trips. Sitting in the Edwardian Tearoom at the Birmingham Museum & Art Gallery, getting my fix of Joan (which is a bit addict-y to be honest) I am transported back when she writes of an incident several years before the death of her husband when *'...I had what I believed at the time to be an apprehension of death...'*. That hit me a bit like a truck. When I have shared my 'forecast', as I named it, with friends who I knew would be able to hear it, it provided a spiritual opportunity for us to contemplate, not by any means something comforting or reassuring, just something else.

About thirty-six hours before I received that call on the 6th of April, I started to develop a creeping discomfort just beneath the ribs on my left-hand side. *No big deal*, I thought, *your back has known worse in its time*. So, on I went, setting up my consulting room for later and then leaving home to attend a Pilates class. But as I walked down the road that leads to Royston Leisure Centre, this feeling in my back both intensified and started to impact a wider area. There were pains in my chest and stomach, not nausea but something spikier and more worrying. So, I stopped, asked myself what the hell I thought I was doing hitting the gym and as a result, headed back home.

Knowing what has always worked for my back-pain *vis a vis* relief, I tried everything I knew and every trick in the book. Nothing. The usual toolkit of stretches, positions and painkillers did nothing. But the pain increased and, knowing that this was not back/body pain as I knew it, I became evermore alarmed. That night, I did not sleep and reluctantly, the next day I cancelled an entire roster of clients, knowing that I simply could not offer what they would need or had a right to expect. Emergency trips to both my GP and osteopath followed. The industrial strength painkillers took the edge off things but not to the extent that the osteopath could touch me or have me bending this way and that to diagnose what was wrong. So tentatively and shuffling like one of the ancients, I returned home, fearing the worst. And all that offered me comfort at this precarious time was the knowledge that if something frightful was headed in my direction, I had at least recently drafted my will and my executors all had copies along with keys to my flat, which I had sent out just weeks earlier. And one of those executors was my brother, who would inherit much of my estate.

That night, my sleep improved and come the morning, the pain had reduced to a throbbing and my chest felt bruised rather than tight. I could walk without every vertebra feeling like it was punching down on a nerve and this instead had been replaced by soreness. By the time I was on the train speeding towards South Dorchester, I did, for one split second, register that the pain had gone.

This forecast or 'apprehension' was not a singular event. If we go with the spiritual flow of things, this was simply the grand finale of something that came upon me in November of the previous year, when a panic attack in the Autumn of 2016, propelled me into action to contact my solicitor. I am well versed in what is sometimes referred to as 'the pathology of the sublime' where us mere mortals suddenly leap upon the spirit bandwagon defensively to help us deal with the terrible and the traumatic. Death, for example. It is, in other words, a delusional, defensive attempt to somehow make things better or, at least, more tolerable when what we really need to be doing is finding a way of sitting with the intolerable.

If this was my very own pathology, then it was a first class fail. It offered me nothing comforting at all. It just did my head in the more I thought about it. It increased the mystery rather than solving anything. But what I do know is that it is, for whatever reason, about something else, which is somehow connected to my brother dying. Anticipation, forecast, psychic telegraphing, a spiritual sneak preview? Who knows? But sometimes, somewhere, you just get a felt sense that something is trying to communicate something to you that really, really matters. Maybe we sometimes receive data from the cosmos because we are super-consciously open to it. I doubt that it's the Almighty pulling our strings and toying with us or the ghost of an ancestor trying to get us to act on a warning and I certainly heard no voice from on high or found myself bathed in celestial light. Just a feeling, just a foretelling, just apprehension.

Cry

All she could taste was salt from her teardrops. It tasted bitter, but she knew this was where she had to start

Pat Schweibert & Chuck DeKlyen
Tear Soup: A Recipe for Healing After Loss

The 2nd of July 2017

I feel as if I am monitoring an experiment and the subject is me. *Subject is functioning on a 'basic needs' plane. However, fluctuations in mood and mobility are increasing but that is not an impingement to impulse buying re: Ralph Lauren dressing gown, located in the John Lewis sale. This may be cause for concern only if this level of consumerism becomes manic.*

Well, the subject is now back at his hotel because he felt spectacularly out of sorts in House of Fraser and, following an 'episode', thought it best.

I always knew, acknowledgement or not, that this break/experiment was going to expose me, once again to the odds, the furies and the elements of my loss and grief. This Sunday morning, secured in my bolthole of choice, the gorgeous 200 Degrees coffee shop on Birmingham's Colmore Row, where Joan and I are beginning our days, I spoke with Roger and said, for the first time 'Oh the relief. I can now be the hot mess of my dreams. No clients, no rituals to host, no immediate plans to put in place. I can now formally fall apart at leisure'. We laughed, not because it was funny but because it was true. What that 'falling apart' might look like on the other hand, is a different matter altogether.

This morning, I woke up crying. I had dreamt of Stewart and it was a mere snapshot of a dream but we were somewhere bland and generic. But I would make a guess that it was Dorchester South station (which is very generic) There was someone with him but I did not recognise or even pay much attention to this figure. I just saw Stewart. I remember the relief at finding him and he did not seem to understand why I was so emotional. But he gave me a hug anyway and I hugged him back, almost collapsing, and said 'I've been having a horrible time'. I wept and he said, 'I know'. Then I woke up.

Not the best set-up for the day but I showered, dressed, took coffee with Joan and then went on an aimless but relaxing amble through the city centre. I have always believed, as I do now, that Virginia Ironside's book *The Rage of Bereavement* is an exceptional, brilliantly researched and bravely personal study of grief and loss. I first read it when my mother died some twenty years ago but I don't really think I was ready to receive it back then, when I was a mere slip of a grieving queen in my thirties. Now, it is one of the many tomes I have embraced and it too forms part of my 'raft'. I treasure my copy (purchased for 1p from Amazon. A bereavement bargain!)

But I have an issue with the *Misery* chapter, where she talks about the different types of crying, the best types, the types to avoid and the fact that some don't cry at all. My problem is that it reads as if there is a choice. I cannot imagine what that would be like in my wildest dreams. Today, walking through a department store to buy candles, reminded me how little choice I actually do have when something needs to erupt, and I say 'erupt' because it does actually feel volcanic in nature.

Within a split second, I felt disoriented and somewhat weak at the knees. I stopped to steady myself on a display, aware and relieved that there was hardly anyone else around. The dizziness abated and while still feeling unsteady, I walked on, confident (really?!?) that this would pass in time. My breathing too felt inconsistent and my surroundings rendered somewhat unreal and even dream-like. I remained convinced that it was a passing thing or maybe the genesis of a silent migraine, which I am prone too. However, next came what I have started to call the 'chest-burster' moment which is a jolting intake of breath or series of quick-fire breaths and always but always precedes a cyclonic tear-drenched meltdown *aka* a grief seizure. So, as this predictably came upon me, I continued on my way, following the path less populated and took the route to the lifts, then down to the ground floor and out into the street.

I checked that I had the emergency meltdown kit – tissues and big sunglasses – and I then let it take its course which it did. It played out with no casualties, no collapse and no panic attack. But at no point do I get even the vaguest sense that I made a choice or that this was just a good old cry. Quite the opposite in fact. These episodes for me have come to feel more like possession and while spinning heads, spewing profanities and projectile vomit have yet to play a part, this almost convulsive manifestation of my grief feels very much how I imagine a demonic infestation might.

Blood

And when your sorrow is comforted (time soothes all sorrows) you will be content that you have known me. You will always be my friend.

Antoine de Saint-Exupéry *The Little Prince*

The 3rd of July 2017

My day began with the mother of all nose bleeds. Nose bleeds are big in my family. This haemorrhage was not, as nose bleeds often are, the result of picking, rubbing or blowing. It just started and within seconds, it had elevated to less of a drip and more of a flow. This was far from perfect timing as it was check-out time in Birmingham, and I was on the clock. But it got me thinking about blood, blood family and bloodletting.

My grandmother was the first in the family to demonstrate the potential the nose holds to let rip and gush. I recall when I was young, walking into the bathroom to find her sitting on the side of the bath and bent forward over the basin, her cream dress and petticoat drenched in blood, a towel pressed against her face. There were streaks of blood in the basin too, but the tap was running, and most had washed away. I remember she looked very scared and deathly pale. It was a horror show. The consequence of this was cauterization later that night in A & E which I had been told involved burning veins to seal them. I think that traumatized me.

I will never know why but when I was I think about 11 or 12, after my grandfather had died from leukaemia, slowly becoming a thinly sketched thing before our very eyes in a ground floor room at my grandparent's house, I was moved in with my grandmother, who lived but half a mile away from the family home. This was an odd and weird move, but I loved my grandmother, found the house both spooky and intriguing and there was an unsettling atmosphere at home, so I simply did as I was told. I remained there for two or three years but we grew to resent one another and eventually my father pulled me from that environment, on the grounds that it he felt it unhealthy for a teenager to be growing up in a house with an old woman. This though is simply an information backdrop to the narrative. While living with my grandmother, I too fell victim to the curse of the nosebleed. On more than one occasion, the bleeds were so ferocious that the only way to stem them was for my grandmother to pack my nostril - it was always the left one - with tightly folded tissue, which often just soaked up the blood and then fell out. The other method was to allow clots to form and then let them harden until the morning when they would then be gently removed.

Our odd relationship with our noses then fell quiet for a short while until two days before my sixteenth birthday. Late afternoon, I experienced another one of those 'It Came from Nowhere' bleeds, when, rather than slowly building up to a gush, this one hit the ground running. Quite literally. I remember cupping my hand underneath my nostril to catch the blood while at the same time running towards the garden where I let it do what it needed to do. The downpour continued for the next thirty minutes and six hours later I was in hospital with transient stroke-like paralysis, a mystery unsolved to this day.

Flash Forward: Two months before Stewart died – and I have no clue if there is any connection – he told me, almost casually, that he had been at the mercy of a two hour unstoppable nasal torrent which eventually took him to hospital, following advice taken from the 111 helpline. When he told me, during his last stay in Royston, I was angry that he had not called me. 'Just didn't think' he had replied. I learned after his death that he had not called his partner either. He just sat there bleeding for two hours. Thinking about that now is no less upsetting than when he first told me.

So, taking the train from Birmingham and bound for the Malvern Hills, I juggle the flashbacks with alacrity and look up just in time as the train passes through the village of Wychbold. And there suddenly to my right is the church, St Mary de Wyche, where my mother's ashes were buried some twenty-one years ago and where I served as head chorister, back in the seventies. Trigger, trigger, trigger, juggle, juggle, juggle.

Climb

Never say goodbye because goodbye means going away and going away means forgetting

J.M. Barrie *Peter Pan*

The 4th of July 2017

In twenty-five formative years, we never went walking on the Malvern Hills. This spectacular part of the landscape, always visible just seventeen miles from the village of Wychbold where Stewart and I both grew up, remained a stranger to us. We may have visited the town of Malvern on occasion – in fact I remember, once; to see a play at the wonderfully broken-down Malvern Festival Theatre, a faded, jaded temple of art that would have hosted the best in its glory days but in the 70's, not so much. It was surely a Norma Desmond amongst provincial theatres. Anyway, the play we came to see was called *The Owl and the Pussycat* and Stewart and I only wanted to see it because Barbra Streisand had starred in the film version. She wasn't in this rendering, so we hated it. Lesson learned.

Why we never took on this awesome range of mountainous mounds and walked it end to end, I'll never know but, for some mysterious reason, I chose this location for my current retreat. And I came here because I simply had an urge, a real appetite to climb them, climb to the top of the highest point and look out over the vast, never-ending shires where we had grown up and simply reflect and remember Stewart and take it all in. This was our land.

But it was also, I believed, an environment free from what Joan Didion describes as *'potentially tricky associations'* because there really was no history, other than the play, to spring out at me. But stepping out of the taxi next to the stairs that led to Malvern Priory, the first thing I see is a shop window, simply choc full of baubles, bangles and beads. If the intention was to stop me in my tracks, then the plan had worked a treat. Tarot cards, fairy lights, tea-light holders in every colour, books stacked high, glass beads strung together by strands of wool and lots and lots of little boxes made from tin, wood, papier-mâché and card. Hello, Stewart, I thought. Again, that word; surrender.

Unsure how, where and when I was going to scale my own private Everest (a little over the top maybe but I don't do inclines normally), I wandered for a time and spent a while inside the Priory. The choir from the local all-girl school nearby was practising in the stalls at the far end and it was quite simply beautiful. So, I sat at the back, deliberately secluding myself in a thinly veiled shadowy nook and lost myself in it all. There were tears, not from distress but remembrance, not pain but love. And the singing grew more intricate as layers of harmony were added and I just could not believe that youngsters were able to make such glorious, rich sounds. I have no idea what they were singing, and I didn't care. My heart was full.

After coffee and deducing from the Malvern Walking app (yes, that's an actual thing) my general direction, I set off. Walking vaguely towards some mid-point, I took the road at the foot of the hills when suddenly to my left the world seemed to open up. I was, in what felt like moments, elevated and looking out over miles and miles of Worcestershire countryside. To my right, the steep banks that formed the sides of the hills got evermore thrilling with rocky ridges, little mysterious pathways and dense forestry stretching up to the sky. I was ecstatic. And it got better. Looking over the sides to the left, revealed extraordinary buildings, homes mainly, built into the stuff of the hillside, with bits and pieces of decking and observation points balanced robustly upon deep rooted legs of steel and wood. Suddenly, I didn't even feel as if I were in this country anymore.

As I made my way around a steep bend, a dead man's curve if ever I saw one, I stumbled upon the portal to the peaks, an easy to miss turn-off called Beacon Road. So, I began my climb. And within minutes I was breathless.

'Stewart, what the fuck am I doing?' I panted. He didn't answer of course but he would have been amused, nonetheless. He was no more a scaler of heights than I was. So what on earth was I doing?

At one point, the woodland to each side fell away and I was hill walking, the slopes now stripped bare and everywhere I turned, the world stretched before me. And then I got it. I knew why I was putting myself through this bizarre and uncharacteristic quest. In the days just after Stewart died when every day felt darker and more broken than the one before, I developed yet another ritual that offered something of a buffer to the blows that were raining down.

I was waking early every day, around five and at one point, rather than just extract myself from the nest of pillows and duvets I had built for myself, only to sit on the edge of the bed for what felt like an age, I pulled on sweatpants, trainers and a hooded top - in fact, Stewart's hooded top - and I walked to the heath. Royston is a small market town and hardly anyone had ever emerged at this point, so I was very much, comfortably alone. It was light but the day was still forming and from the edge of the heath, I could see at its highest point, the old bench, dilapidated and a bit wonky but welcoming, nonetheless. Soon, I was there, sitting, watching, questioning, talking to Stewart, crying like it was my first time and observing all things from above. And that, for some reason, felt just a tad safer. And so, my daily sojourn was born.

'So you do know', Stewart would say, 'you do know why on this day you have scaled the Malvern Hills to their highest point?' And I would say 'yes, I do'. 'So, what do you know?' he would ask. And I would reply, as I spun round at the height of heights, taking in the world 'Stop asking bloody questions and let's just enjoy the view'. And smiling, we do.

Reunion

What we have once enjoyed deeply we can never lose. All that we love deeply becomes a part of us.

Helen Keller

The 7th of July 2017

While the taxi journey to the Woodlands Burial Grounds gave not an inkling of the seismic rumbles to come – this was, I recalled in a moment, my first return since the day of the service so really what did I expect? – it took just one step inside that nondescript, farm shop inspired woodland reception room before I was time travelled back to the 5th of May, local time 15:00 hours. I kept company with these red, raw and dripping memories while I waited. Funeral director Richard was occupied and giving, as I am sure he always does, undivided attention to an elderly man in sorrowful, mid-reminiscence about a lost loved one (I came to understand that it was his wife he had come to 'visit'). Feeling slightly awkward, as if I'd just interrupted someone's actual funeral, I sat and tried to look invisible but it's hard to be inconspicuous with a rucksack and a red wheelie suitcase. So, I just sat very still and terribly quiet.

Then, as the man left and Richard turned his attention to me, shaking my hand oh so firmly, I was gripped by the full force of another ripple of grief. The body remembers, as they say, and mine was now somehow suddenly confused as I went through the motions of our first meeting once again – the greeting, the handshake, the offer of tea. Fuck, I could hear my body ask with fear in its loins, is history repeating itself? Starting to sweat, my breathing all out of sync and barely able to get a word out that sounded like, well, a word, Richard simply asked again 'Cup of tea?' to which I nodded yes. At least, I could still nod. I made the kind of speedy dash to the toilet one undertakes when vomit is on the cards. However, in this case, it was to release the tear demon, allow the moaning and convulsions to abate and then, restored, try all that again.

When I returned, the tea was brewing and a small luxury bag with rope handles sat beside the mug. Richard placed his hand gently upon the package.

'I just want to check that the plaque is up so can I leave you with this?' he said.

'Of course,' I replied, knowing full well what was in it.

'You'll be OK?'

Stop it. You're scaring me, I thought. 'Sure. Sure I will' I said instead. And with that, he smiled and disappeared out into the burial grounds.

I looked at the bag and began to untie the knot in the rope handles. Reaching inside, I lifted out the robust but short cardboard tube container and popped off the plastic top. Then I hesitated. That weird breathing thing started to happen again, so I did my comfort ritual – slow breath out and gentle pat on chest. Moving on.

Gently pulling at the drawstring to open the black velvet bag, I was struck by how heavy the contents were. I had imagined something smaller and certainly lighter. Placing one hand gently beneath, the other reached in and gently extracted the large glass orb. I held it up and observed the swirls of dancing colour inside. And there he is. There is Stewart. Not a memory of Stewart or a signification or a representation but actual Stewart, little tiny pieces of pearlised ash suspended forever in a protective glass sphere. I am enthralled. Hi Stewie, I say in my head.

Intimacy

Wake up in the morning and what do you see? Death. Open the door. Death. Answer the phone? Death. It crowds around you, pressing in, whispering 'I'm here, I'm here, I'm here…'

Virginia Ironside *You'll Get Over It: The Rage of Bereavement*

The 10th of July 2017

Simply by the nature of things, the 'three acts' as I have come to call them – the cremation, the interment of Stewart's ashes and the celebration of life – could only provide a thinly sketched idea of my sense of people just as they, in turn, could only grasp fleetingly a passing sense of me. Not wholly accurate come to think of it as I did choose the maximum exposure option as centre-stage host on these three occasions (as in, I could have handed it over to someone else) but nonetheless, I had painstakingly scripted the events for damage limitation purposes.

So, this weekend was to be very different and actually far more exposing. It was the weekend of the apartment clear-out and many had been invited to help, to take a memento or two or simply to express love and pay respect to Stewart, sans all the formal trappings of ceremony. My neuroses had been flexing their collective muscles for some days now – would the approval rating slide? Would they find me a pale imitation, a phoney, a fake? Would they slump into a dismissive position where I became actually, not very impressive at all? No wonder I started to twitch with panic when, days earlier, I strode up the Malvern Hills, noticed a hawk about to descend upon its prey and wondered if that would be me come the weekend. Projection, grief and vulnerability are clearly a heady mix of mind-fuckery but fortunately, it did not take long for me to re-calibrate to a more balanced position. In other words, I kindly, and with love, encouraged myself to get a bloody grip.

Saturday in Bournemouth began very much as I imagined it would continue. I rose early – around 6am – stared out across that familiar stretch of sea, showered and dressed groggily and by 6.45, I was walking the deserted streets from East Overcliff Drive to Lansdowne Road. Dread made my head rattle and panic felt like it was entering standby mode. The first part of my morning, when I had decided I needed to be alone to pack up Stewart's clothes, had begun.

The flat was very much as I remembered it, all a bit random and hodge podge. Things just plonked down here and there and all very much in the freestyle of my brother. I loved it and I hated it too. But I did not dawdle and, armed with extra strong plastic sacks, I moved to the bedroom. Before I began, I prepared a number of bags and then remembered that I should probably go around opening all the windows because it was going to be hot and the flat needed to be aired through. It was, come to think of it, rather musty when I opened the front door. That done, I wondered if I should have tea first. *Stephen, stop stalling, start packing.*

I take down a shirt. I start to fold it. It's a blue retro style 50's short sleeve number. I have one identical. We bought them together in the Next sale in 2014 when Stewart came to stay in Royston. I floated off somewhere as I began to cry, and tears went everywhere. Not a good start. I try again with a striped jumper. He used to wear this with a T-shirt underneath, very much known as a signature Stewart look. I begin to crumble fast. I walk out of the room, gasping and make my way to the kettle, dabbing at the snot and saltwater as I go. I make that cup of tea and stand near the window, lace curtains wafting lightly and sun hitting the floor through the side glass of the bay alcove. I have a gentle word with myself. *My good man, if you don't want to be doing this for the next week, find a way. This is awful. Let it be awful.*

So I let it be. I think I had gone too far the other way, the place where denial hangs out. I was internally circulating that 'Oh, it'll be fine' memo for days prior to arrival, bullshitting myself that it will, you know, be part of the healing process. Well, it won't be, and it doesn't have to be. And with that, armed with English Breakfast char and a granola bar, I began the almost religious task of gently and lovingly folding all my brother's pressed shirts and freshly laundered jeans and jumpers into ten very full plastic sacks. I had found my next ritual.

Orb

Brother, were I a teardrop I would fall like flooded waters
For the deep limits of sorrow's tears are not yet found

Traditional Indian Elegy

The 13th of July 2017

10:17am – I now have a little piece of Stewart immortalised for all time in that tennis ball sized glass sphere. I show it proudly to good friends and allies, to those who will understand, to those who will not think it the most ghoulish thing ever to have ashen particles of my brother frozen inside a lump of glass.

Already, I am talking to it, chatting away casually or deep in conversation at least once a day. 'Stewart' I say 'if I have you on the mantelpiece, I am going to FREAK OUT every time I walk past or someone else does' And so I'm on Amazon within seconds (Amazon is having a boom time with my bereavement) and faster than you can say ashes into glass, I have ordered something called a glass cloche bell jar. A bamboo base, upon which stands a perfectly formed curved cover, will soon house my memorial to Stewart (or more precisely, de-constructed Stewart) and, just as I feel relieved that I can now keep it more securely contained, I also feel ambivalent and hesitant. What the hell am I doing, I wonder, what is this really all about?? In my quandary, I drift towards a belief that I am finding methods by which to deny, to skirt around or just ignore the hard and horrible fact of death (which is, after all, the most defining hard and horrible fact of life for me at this time). I also don't think I care. I treasure my orb. Maybe at some point a friend or group of loved ones will perform an intervention, tough loving me back to reality and forcing me to suffer grief and loss cold turkey and confiscating the item 'for my own good'.

I am mesmerised by the swirl of ruby red flame that lies at the heart of the ball, that looks at once like both fire and the unfurling bud of a strange flower. And there, attached to the outside edge of every dancing petal, I see Stewart, each ash particle transformed magically into a pearly bubble, suspended, it would seem, in space. It is a thing of wonder.

'We, us humans, are creatures of ritual and symbols' I remember saying at the celebration of life. But what will this symbolise? Is this just another distraction, something to assuage the wrenching loss for a short while longer, a desperate clinging to some manufactured bauble that I'm foolish enough to believe is somehow alive, that somehow means that Stewart did not die how he died on the 6th of April 2017? I sort of don't think so. An appraisal of Joan Didion's book, that I have referenced with something of a relentless fixation, draws attention to the part material possessions play in her narrative and how crucial they become to meaning reconstruction for the bereaved. And as I consider that, a penny loudly drops. It is that it means something to me. It influences me not to believe that Stewart is alive but that this beautiful, wondrous thing only came into being because he is not. Like the glass itself, that much is crystal clear. I would trade one for the other at the drop of a handbag, but that option is not available. To me, it represents eternal things and how all things are conjoined. I stare into its ruby red heart and I feel loss, but I also feel love. I'm gripped by anguish but also beauty. I sense devastation but also devotion. It represents part of my story, my extraordinary, complicated relationship with the brother who died like a bolt out of the blue, leaving me weeping, wailing, gnashing my teeth and ordering glass memorials from a glossy catalogue. It is, then, all things and it means everything to me.

Clench

No matter how many rainbows and butterflies you stick into the narrative, some stories just don't work out.

Megan Devine *It's OK That You're Not OK*

The 14th of July 2017

To be honest, most quotes, poems and prayers claiming to be about grief and loss really piss me off. I read them and they get 'the look'. Apparently, they're meant to be inspirational and I was inspired on several occasions - inspired to throw the fucking book across the room and scream. But every now and then, I happen upon something that just rings bells for me. Not some nonsense along the lines of Henry Scott Holland's famous verse:

Death is nothing at all.
I have only slipped away to the next room.

Nothing at all? Oh right, well, I guess I must be making all this pain and torment up then because I've got nothing better to do. So shut the fuckity fuck up!

And relax. But that's what this kind of grief 'gift-wrapping' does to me these days, I'm afraid. That said, the winds of change have clearly blown through over the years because it was exactly this verse I once embraced with gusto and read out at my mother's funeral some twenty years ago. So, I guess I should shut the fuckity fuck up as well then. Fair cop.

But time has ticked by, and the sands shifted because I really perked up when I read this by history author Mary Hollingsworth:

Love is stronger than death
So, I must be content to know that
Love is not affected by death
It doesn't end, it doesn't diminish
It doesn't change

And I perked up for the simple reason that I believe it. I have often said that death is not so bold that it can change or annihilate love. Her words may not offer me comfort. But they do speak a truth. And that's a lot.

Landscapes

You need the reality of your loss reflected back to you – not diminished, not diluted.

Megan Devine It's OK That You're Not OK

The 15th of July 2017

Today, I attended a training and education day, one of several I had booked back in March, which, as fate would have it, was all about, yes, that's right, grief and loss.

Feeling somewhat touch-and-go about the whole thing, I took to Facebook to share a moment, writing *'I booked this back in March. It will be either spookily timely or the worst decision I've made in the last three months'*. It turned out to be more the former (and maybe a little bit the latter but nothing is ever that cut and dried)

In the presence of over one hundred therapists – like me, several were very recently bereaved – the facilitators of the conference, two prolific voices in the 'field' took to the stage to get the grief ball rolling. Next, a geographer (a what where?!?) presented material that I wanted to write off from the get-go, seeking to dismiss it with a bat of the hand as a tall order or stretching it a bit until I found a hundred snapshots and flashbacks pinging off in my head like special effects. Referencing places and spaces, the sea, the shoreline, memorial benches, stones and plaques, the presentation illustrated how we engage with our environment as we memorialise, honour, receive and in return release the dead. Everything, I did, in fact for Stewart, for me, for his friends. *Note to self:* try listening with an open mind. You might just learn something.

But this day also reminded me that stumbling blocks, threats and dangers can come from the most unexpected places and people when one is bereaved. It's painful to find out that our unrealistic expectation that the world will reconfigure around our grief and pain is simply not to be. On this day of days, it was when author/screenwriter B took to the spotlight that I was reminded of my earlier ambivalence about attending. Spookily timely or worst decision? I was about to find out.

As psychotherapist and celebrated writer, Mr A took his seat to discuss Mr B's latest work via a conversation with the author himself, it was apparent that the scribe was not present. He was held up, we were told, and on his way. So A improvised on the popular theme of grief and threw likely controversy into the proceedings by quoting the 19th century American poet Ralph Waldo Emmerson, who wrote, having lost his son to scarlet fever '...*the only thing grief has taught me, is to know how shallow it is...*'. A appeared to support this view, as did the 'late' Mr B who, having since arrived, then also dissed the idea of both soul and meaning to boot. There was no challenge from the crowd, not even from me. I just sat there, feeling my grief and thinking of my brother. Maybe they were telling those in the room, some dripping with their own loss that they were phoney, that they, the academics, knew better than us and that we were kidding ourselves. And maybe, due to their undeniable charisma, we were being led to believe they were right, and we were wrong. Or I'm in some blind, narcissistic grief state taking everything *very* personally. Whatever.

During the final session, reflections and stories which we had written down on paper earlier and placed in a box were read out for consideration and reflection in the last hour. As one of our 'hosts' turned to the inevitable issue of our own vulnerability and reached for a piece of paper in front of her, my heart did something. 'I'll just read this' she said ' "*Following the recent and sudden death of my younger brother, I find myself currently not only in the blast zone of my own grief but daily with clients entering their own* "'I had written this earlier and placed it in the tray with many others, unsure how, if it were chosen, it would be incorporated. She read it like it really mattered, she read it with respect, she read it knowing that grief is a bottomless pit. No one knew those were my words. They didn't need to. They just needed to know that they were someone's truth and far, far from shallow.

Imagine

Siblings are reference points, and we often gauge where we are in life with comparison to them.

Elizabeth DeVita-Raeburn
The Empty Room: Understanding Sibling Loss

The 17th of July 2017

Imagine swimming for days, for weeks, months even, in grief-infested waters. Imagine looking every which way and seeing nothing, not even a passing chunk of debris or flotsam. So you flail and spit and breathe and gasp, wide-eyed and weighed down. Imagine absorbing more and more of this ocean of despair, soaking it up like a sponge. Surely, you think, you're just stalling the inevitable. Surely you will at some point just drown.

And then, you see rocks. You make your way towards them and haul yourself on to the crag. Now you can see it all but you're not in it. It clings to you, you are surrounded by it but you are not being dragged down. You see your brother in the chapel of rest, the tubes, the star tattoos. You see people crying in a woodland, rose petals and you hear music. The violin and the piano. Deep beneath the surface, something blurry but still recognizable to you; an estranged brother. And as you cast your eye further, over the endless depths, everywhere you turn, fifty-seven years of family stretches out in every direction.

What you do not see, is the mounting tsunami coming at you from behind because all you can know is how a small passage of time has given you just this modest crag to cling to, to climb upon. And for a moment at least, the undercurrents of grief are not pulling at you, eating you up, ripping you limb from limb.

But then that wave hits. This morning, back at the coal face of work, wisps of the 6th of April hung in the air, little fluttering things all around me. I had made tea as I prepared for a Skype session with Jenna and, as I walked into the living room (*aka* my consulting room), tectonic plates shifted and the quake hit. I'm mixing my metaphors here, I know, so take your pick. Blind-sided by something awe-inspiring, I was back in the chapel, standing by my brother, choked and churning like it was happening now. I stopped, I placed the tea down before I dropped it and remember saying 'What the fuck?'. Flashback: The chapel of rest (or land of the dead. Again, take your pick): I'm looking at his slightly turned head. Flashback: Close-up on the reddish-purple impact injury. I gasp. Flashback: I'm holding his hand. I can't wake him up. I can't keep him safe. I have failed him. The quake/wave thing arrives. Something has caught up with me.

It's all a familiar narrative these days. Collapse, weep, repeat. It is a truism, however, that it never feels the same twice. Every collapse is its own unique creation. So, when some people ask of the grieving *aren't you over it by now?*, they have clearly never been there (and may the universe help them if and when they do). It might look the same, but it never, never feels it.

I was very frightened today. It shocked me. I collapsed into a nightmare and it felt quite mad. And it will probably happen again, and I don't know when. I don't know why it is or how it is. I just need to know that it is. Because my brother still is dead, and it still is terrible. It just is. And so for now, I'll just drink my tea.

Unknown

Siblings know each other in ways other friends and other blood relatives do not. We have shared bathrooms, bedrooms, holidays, school days, family milestones, meals and a way of growing up that people outside the family do not understand.

Brenda J. Marshall *Sibling Loss Across the Lifespan*

The 19th of July 2017

In the week I return to work, following my period of leave, tests and challenges abound, not least stepping back into the counsellor/supervisor role, about which I must say I feel very ambivalent. As to why, well, that'll just have to wait. But as I take the bus to Cottenham to attend the hospice in the line of my work, I am pre-occupied with the stuff of family.

I knew Stewart and Stewart knew me. To each other and in our adult years, we had become 'known' family while others in the family system - mother, father and eldest sibling - remained in many ways always and forever unrevealed, somewhat masked, somehow thinly sketched and deeply incongruent. But what now? Stewart has gone. He has died. There is no more known family. That's it. It's over, it's gone, period. Is that the instigator of my loneliness? It certainly isn't as a result of neglect from others. Not a bit of it. The people I love and who have been there from the first moment I entered the maelstrom, ready to literally catch me should I fall, remain as constant as ever. They are fearless and present figures in my life, attending to me constantly as I slip and slide between crazy, restored, devastated and sometimes doing not bad at all. Some of this because of my grief and much in spite of it. But the loneliness I have felt since packing up the Bournemouth flat has stirred something else altogether.

I feel a bit like Bette Midler's wretched and wrecked rocker, Rose at the end of the film of the same name when, as she succumbs to drug induced death, she looks up, eyes half closed and, with what little will she can muster says *'Where ya goin'? Where's everybody goin'?'* Because everybody has gone. I look around and sure enough, I don't know anyone else from either side of the family. No aunts, uncles, nephews, nieces, half this or half that. Sure, the estranged brother made a decision to attend the funeral day, but he is not known to me and what I do know of him, a patchwork of painful memories, full of judgement, rejection and threat, just makes me recoil. If anything, he simply reminds be how alone I really am, in terms of lineage. I hate that he is my only touchstone and it bangs it home to an even greater extent, just how much it meant to me that Stewart and I shared planet earth together and how I miss just knowing he is somewhere out there as flesh and blood, *my* blood. Fifty-two years of stuff. Who the hell will I talk to now about fifty-two years of stuff that only we know? It's like half the planet fell away.

So, it's a barren family plain I occupy these days with just me for company, apart from a lock of hair, an orb, some ashes in a plastic bag and the clothes of the dead. I still cannot bring myself to open the hospital bag, that scary, green, crinkly plastic thing that contains the clothes my brother died in. Maybe that is yet another pretty thinly disguised denial strategy. I'd like to say that it represents the last vestige of Stewart's alive-ness and that to open it finally would be to let death out of the bag. But that doesn't sound at all convincing, just gobbledygook. I guess at some point I just need to open that bag.

Avoidance

Another condolence no-no is to make false promises or statements that on the surface sound very caring and sincere but are really just fluff

T.J. Wray *Surviving the Death of a Sibling*

The 20th of July

It could be said – and it often is – that grief is one of the most profound journeys upon which any of us will ever embark. While never chosen, it is however inevitable, one of those existential realities that is so often omitted from the 'givens' list.

What also seems inevitable is that other 'given' otherwise known as 'the shit people say'. Virginia Ironside's book *You'll Get Over it: The Rage of Bereavement* takes one of those clichés and turns it into the first half of her title. As I stood in the kitchen earlier this evening, final supervisee supervised, salad tossed and two fresh vases of flowers arranged and placed (it's become my homage to my brother it would seem and I channel him to perfection as I get all OCD about balancing the blooms and making the right shape. It used to drive me nuts), I spoke to the space around me, saying 'Stewart, I think you'd probably rise above. I think you'd give the benefit of the doubt, but those things people say, well, I give very short shrift'

There have been those 'moments of truth' over the past three months but my defences were piqued just this week, when, on the cusp of a squat pre-Pilates, a woman I barely know, came bouncing over to me with an air of mania, smiling like a Florida waitress and weirdly wide-eyed like someone just said 'Frown and I'll shoot'. All flaming red lipstick and rictus grin, she asked 'So are you on the up then?'. As she said 'up', she did this odd gesture with both hands as if slapping the air. 'Am I what?' I asked. I found her invasion of my space a bit disturbing. She repeated and doubled down 'On the up? Are you on the up??' I took a beat. 'Oh, you mean in the light of my younger brother suddenly dropping dead three months ago at the age of fifty-two?'. She actually genuinely thought I was just clarifying for the sake of actually genuinely clarifying. 'Yes' she said 'Well, are you?'. I didn't answer so she continued. 'I lost my husband at 49' Pause 'I was in the wilderness for two years' And before you could say dust to dust, she'd turned on her Pilates plimsolls and retreated back to her mat where she started to do technically questionable roll-downs before the class had even started. I simply gawped, feeling no compunction to offer her comfort or a get-out clause. As I said, short shrift.

This is so often the best the avoidant types can muster. Other humdingers include 'How do you know life will never be the same?', 'Well, I hope I go like that', 'You OK then?', 'Well, at least he didn't suffer' and the apologist for the avoidants 'I'm sure they're just trying to help'. With responses that range from the naive (also known as plain fucking stupid) to the spectacularly narcissistic (the ones that somehow manage to make my brother's death about them), it's a wonder there isn't blood on the walls on a daily basis. However, the plain, simple reason I am not currently serving life for homicide, has more to do with my effective strategies for avoiding the avoidants most of the time but sometimes, when the planets align, they just have you cornered.

The most curious thing is why they would choose to approach in the first place. What compels them to do this remains a mystery. I simply cannot fathom why someone would make a conscious decision to walk up to the recently bereaved, a virtual stranger and say 'I've heard. I do hate seeing you like this'. The solution to that one is simple – in that case, don't 'see' me and don't walk up to me. Problem, as they say, solved.

Wilderness

Those left behind face an uncharted future afloat the perilous seas of powerlessness

Virginia Ironside *You'll Get Over It: The Rage of Bereavement*

The 24th of July 2017

So, what is this then? Does this even have a name? Is there a part of the process called the 'wilderness' stage because that's what it feels like? Or maybe it could be called the critical/angry/self-harm/bitchy/shade-throwing stage? No, that doesn't have a nifty ring to it. I guess I'll just have to inhabit the wilderness for a while and see what transpires, with all its slippery-slidey, upsey-downsey, jiggery pokery.

The end of yesterday continued its descent into a morass of rage, self-loathing, shame and weeping. It grew late and as I sponged and lathered away at a bowl of dirty mugs and crockery, the salty 'sweat' from my eyes just drip-drip-dripped into the bubbles and murky water. I carried on unphased by this but heavy of heart and mind. I just didn't get what all this surging anger was all about, a rampaging animosity both towards others and myself? Is this what Virginia Ironside describes as the bereaved's '... *random discharges of unfocused rage...* ? So many questions.

The tears made it hard to focus and as I placed a mug onto the drainer, I chipped it and it took all my restraint (and then some) to stop me back handing it and propelling it across the kitchen. That was a frightening splurge of anger right there. Cue a sense of collapse. Fury and then powerlessness.

I have not transformed my apartment into a shrine to my brother but today is a raw time and I miss him terribly and I want to see and be in the company of all the mementos I saved from his home. I have to catch myself more and more when, in moments that find me flirting with denial, I think 'Oh I must remember to tell Stewart this or that' or 'I haven't phoned Stewart lately. I'll do it now'. But, like I say, I catch myself and I don't of course scribble memos or dial the dead.

But it is now nearly four months from the day Stewart died and I sense some friends have adjusted expectations of me even if I haven't. I may well be projecting like the grieving benchmark that I am but I do get the sense from some – more colleagues than friends to be really accurate – that they cannot be with me in this as they were last month, the month before and the month before that. I do not blame them. I just know it's true. And so, following the usual disturbed night, I think about this as I prepare for my 8am client. But projection or not, I still feel out of sorts regardless. It's just a hefty lump of weird, wrapped up in crazy and topped off with a big fancy bow of odd. I don't like it and I don't like me. I frustrate myself not knowing what to call this part of the journey. I'm scanning all the books I've read, now stored in the brain library, hoping to happen upon a quote, a chapter, a pithy one-liner or a case example but I am at a loss.

I want to criticise others (or perhaps be downright mean) but I fear criticism myself. The smallest dose feels like shaming humiliation. I fend it off with anger as something in my head repeatedly tells the world and everyone in it to just fuck off. Of course, I censor and silence myself politely and sort of just embrace the day. And with a day of supervisees and clients ahead of me, I brace myself with a 'fake it till you make it' resolve. But who am I to offer containment and support when I feel barely able to bestow it upon myself? Wow, what a phoney! But, forewarned is forearmed and while I'm hardly going to win Therapist of the Year, I continue to 'bracket' like my life depends upon it (maybe it does) and the day passes without fight, flight or freeze.

So welcome to the Wilderness, that uncharted terrain that almost defies definition or description. I'm all anxious, neurotic, messy, dramatic and overwrought. But I'm playing to an audience of just one. Me. But that's OK. This one will run for years.

Oblivion

Grievers use a very simple calendar. Before and after.

Lynda Cheldelin Fell & Christine Bastone
Grief Diaries: Surviving Loss of a Sibling

The 27th of July 2017

I may own a flat in the middle of a town, but this is a market town and as such it is relatively quiet for a townscape come 11pm. But I'm not quiet as I lie here under the duvet. That's 'not quiet' as in unsettled, not at peace, restless and perturbed. Very not quiet. So, I turn on my white noise machine for company and look around the tome-strewn bed and I think what now? Just that. *What now??*

I think I dreaded more than anything the infamous depressive slump, the feeling that you could just collapse in on yourself, your head sinking between your shoulder blades as you deflate into folds of flesh. Meaning and purpose become notions just too elusive and exhausting to contemplate, life's many colours and textures just wash away, leaving stains and outlines behind and everything becomes a bigger effort with every breath. Being is an effort, living is an effort, even pissing is an effort. *Please can I just die.* But let me compose the order of service for my funeral and disseminate copies of my will first. Got to get the priorities right.

Also, this is not the land of spiky anxiety, all sweat and heightened emotion. No, this is vapid, limp and flaccid. It's that thing we dread. Limbo, a sort of non-being. It feels like the place you go to when, after you have straddled the divide between those two lands week after week after week, you simply cannot hold yourself up any longer and the nothing-ness sucks you down. You no longer straddle but instead collapse into it. I'm there.

Motivation seems like a luxury item and drive or passion simply the stuff of fantasy. I don't know how I feel about much really. I'm emotionally flat lining before my very eyes. But I do my work, I eat my dinner and I pop a cork on a bottle of Merlot, simply as a matter of habit. The Merlot thankfully still hits the spot. The anguish is dulled, the devastation reduced, the overwhelm on hold. I just don't feel much of anything and yet I see Stewart, sense Stewart and talk with Stewart no less. But is he vanishing? Is he less than he was last week, last month, on the 6th of April? Oh God, this feels like hell but the boring version. So here I lie on my bed surrounded by books about grief, sibling loss and how to live with grief after a sudden death. Together, they form a great big comfort blanket of pages and sweet words. And they're all for me I think narcissistically. And I say in my silence, Stewart, don't leave me. I reach for a book – *The Empty Room* by Elizabeth DeVita-Raeburn – and I read, hoping I'll find him hiding among the chapters and words. *Stewart, don't leave me, don't leave me, don't leave*...Oh you already did. I'm terrified of forgetting. I know this happens because my comfort blanket of books tells me so time and time again. But still I'm terrified that Stewart is slipping between my fingers and things are moving on. Surely, there's another ritual to plan, to create, to host. Maybe I'll invent one. Anything.

But no. No sooner do I surrender to the inevitability of waking up every day for the rest of my life, staring into the jaws of death than something much worse comes thundering towards me in the night and the rules of engagement change again. Anguish, desolation, terror, madness: at least you know where you are with those emotions. But this, this is unformed, shapeless and remote. And then suddenly I get it. I have no sense of anything and for the first time in nearly four months, I don't really have a sense of me.

Welcome to oblivion.

Disenfranchised

Disenfranchised grief can end up in what (in the language of loss) is known as "complicated mourning" – grief that, unexpressed and unexplored, takes on an unhealthy form.

Elizabeth DeVita-Raeburn
The Empty Room: Understanding Sibling Loss

The 31st of July 2017

Apparently, I'm disenfranchised. I don't feel disenfranchised but according to research on sibling loss, it is often so defined, taking its place alongside the loss experience of mistresses (and the male equivalent too I presume) LGBTQ partners (out and otherwise) and those in relationships where religion and culture play a key role. Even bereavement has a pecking order.

But I do understand the idea of disenfranchised grief as it relates to the death of a sibling but for me, I have managed to completely avoid this familial impotence for one simple reason. The competition is dead. According to the written word, it is most common for the sympathy focus to go to, amongst others, parents and children of the deceased. And so that's why I'm not side-lined. There are no distractions and true, over time, during the last four months, as week after week after week passed by sometimes in a flash, sometimes with such inertia that I felt as if I too must have expired, this loss of my brother has felt exclusively my domain, mine to own and mine alone. And, bottom line, in 'blood' terms, that's no lie.

When I entered that agonizing scene back in April, clinging to anything in the world that could give me an anchor, there was from the very beginning of things a sense that I was significant in this. I felt it from all the people I met, spoke with, embraced, clung to, sat with and wept alongside. I was

Stewart's brother, the brother and there was no one else. I wonder if this is thinly veiled conceit, an arrogance or a need to be needed but if it is, then, hey, whatever. To lead the way both for myself and so many others in the wake of such horror and shock felt like a sort of unspoken understanding, a silent contract between us all.

While nobody in Stewart's world really knew me on the 6th of April – I had met but a handful of Stewart's nearest and dearest previously – slowly but surely, as word spread from the few to the many, I never felt less than wholeheartedly respected and honoured as the only one who could and even should bring all things together. And oddly, I experienced a felt sense that they truly trusted me to do so (or felt they had little option). Of course, wishful thinking is a wonderful thing, but I'll go with it anyhow. Knowing, as I do now with hindsight, that what I tirelessly worked towards for Stewart, with a lot of love and a somewhat obsessive-compulsive eye for the minutiae of all things funereal, was actually a group act of love. Because nobody – and I mean nobody – was going to feel disenfranchised on my watch.

If the books I read are anything to go by, it is not ever thus for all siblings. I have been fortunate. From all corners, both among my chosen family and that of my brother, my loss has been handled with kid-glove care and consideration by practically everyone I have encountered in the aftermath of all this. Not by over-attending, happy facing, cheering me, mollycoddling or some such but in silence, reflection, a look, a connection or a touch. Sometimes, that's all it takes.

Lull

Grief is part of love.

Megan Devine *It's OK That You're Not OK*

The 2nd of August 2017

August descends with the inevitable lull in proceedings. School holidays arrive amidst dismal, sloppy weather and the rain sweeps in and out, attempting oh so successfully to catch us off guard by every now and then teasing with a sneak peek of blue skies and sun. The mischief is successful - we're all bamboozled into leaving home without umbrellas. We never learn and we pay the price. The relentless soaking however comes this Summer with uncharacteristic high winds that up the wind chill factor considerably.

I am grateful for the dip in work demands and already know how I will be filling the extra time I have to hand. I will refine my will and I will write out the order of the day for my funeral from the moment news of my death will be broken right through to the apportioning of my belongings, otherwise known in the trade as 'the chattels'. At the same time, the joke is also on me because I won't be around to direct proceedings according to 'the script'.

So, I have begun to literally put my house in order, and all of this triggered by the latest of my 'rituals'. It's clearly not done with me yet, all this ritual rigmarole. I had never heard of anyone creating a memory box until a supervisee at the hospice mentioned it in the line of our work together. For days I just could not get it out of my head and then it came to me; I will create two memory boxes, one for Stewart and one for myself. They will contain the most personal items from our lives, be they baubles, bangles or beads, sketches, scribbles or souvenirs. And I will place them in two simple boxes, purchased of course especially for this exercise and they will live in the attic, side by side, Stewart and me.

I had wondered for an age what to do with those special but practically extraneous bits and pieces that belonged to my brother; an empty mint tin, some spectacle wipes, his phone, the canvas shoulder bag he had with him the day he died. I would never use them, but I could not throw them away. Then, as I began to redraft my own will, taking inventory of my apartment and culling as I went, my supervisee's idea re-occurred to me.

And so it begins. I slowly begin to fill my memory box with oddities and little marvels, which include the toe tag from the day I was born and a tiny baby vest, apparently mine from 1959. Then photos of my grandmother's house, my grandmother, my parents' wedding and various pictures of me performing. Theatre programmes from *Aspects of Love* at the Prince of Wales Theatre, the TV section of *OK* magazine with me on the cover and a newspaper from the day I was born, a gift from friends for my 50th birthday. The whole past, present and future whirlwind sweeps me off my feet. And then I land with a thud. Amidst the dusty collection of papers, I find death certificates. I lift out my mother's and relive the day of her death in five seconds. *Night, phone call, rain, hospital, body, more rain.* Then my father's and the same mind-warp erupts. *Sun, sea, phone-call, shock, journey, home.* Now you have three death certificates, I say to myself, and two of them bear your signature.

I look at Christmas cards that I saved. I find one with a retro 50's style design, all bright colours and shiny triangles with 50's Optima font wishing me Merry Christmas. It can only be from one person. I open it and read – *Steve...to my lovely brother...Much Love & Every best wish for a satisfying 2017! Stewart xxx.* And I think 'Well, it was satisfying...and then you died'. That's the last card my brother will ever send me. I close it and place it carefully in my memory box like it's made of glass.

So I've got a lot done this week I must say, but most importantly I have my memory boxes and as I look at them before flicking off the loft light, two gift boxes brimming over with stuff utterly meaningless to anyone other than Stewart and me, I feel very, very close to him.

'Night, Stew', I say out loud.

And with a flick, darkness.

Screaming

Grief is not like the measles; and you don't recover from it and go back to being the person you were before you suffered the bereavement. We are all permanently changed by grief. But the changes which take place need not be changes for the worse

Colin Murray Parkes *The Price of Love*

The 5th of August 2017

It has been quite the week. I have crossed a line. I am falling.

With the familiar snap, snap, snap at my heels as I moved from 'I must get organised' to 'Quick before you die' (that's the line crossing part), my sense of restoring order amidst the tumbling, rumbling grief turned into a manic race against time. I somehow convinced myself that the memory boxes, the antique valuations and the writing of wills, funeral arrangements and therein the dissemination of all that I own, were in fact a series of cryptic messages from the cosmos telling me that I, too, was about to die without warning.

In a busy week of clients in mourning, on the cusp of relapse or staring into the abyss, this was also the week that Stewart's pension fund provider ruled on the death benefit (why does that just sound so wrong? Death *benefit*??) and, as I had surmised, the decision made to split the sum equally between myself and the estranged brother. It was inevitable and yet represented one more thing from which I yearned to escape. How fucking *dare* he make any kind of gain from Stewart's death. I am sick to my stomach thinking about it. I hope it kills him, says the shadow.

Good. OK. Moving on.

And in this frenzied yet weirdly high-functioning state, I felt drawn and driven back to my bench on the heath. With the flat in disarray as a result of my manic carry-on, looking now like the aftermath of some ferocious paranormal activity, I stomped out of the apartment which suddenly felt hideously airless. Without a second thought, I made my way along the main road until I reached the cusp of the golf course. I struggled to breathe and wondered if this was the clock ticking towards my final moments. Then, a bit of something stirring, a memory, a recollection. I was suddenly walking the same path I took with Stewart some three years ago. I remember it because we were mildly traumatized having witnessed the beautiful butterflies that covered the grasslands repeatedly and compulsively drawn to the carelessly neglected dog faeces that littered the track. Our joy turned from 'Oh how enchanting' as they floated around us to 'Filthy bastards!' as they came into land.

But I could not find our bench. The seat that we sat on to view across the heath, an elevated area that looked directly across to that other bench of more recent visits, seemed to have gone. I became overwrought. I began spluttering up grief and tears and words, muttered and mumbled as I tramped through the long grass in search. It was almost as if I expected to find Stewart sitting there, if I could only find the bench. Ergo, I MUST find it. And then suddenly, there it was.

But Stewart, of course, was not there. So, I sat alone with all my stuff going on, realizing too late that I had nothing with which to mop up the nasal and watery discharge. Lots of wiping and sniffing ensued as a consequence, while I sat in stillness and the glorious evening sun.

This week I have spent serious time communing with the dead. I have revisited the deaths of my father, my mother and my brother by relentlessly sifting through, examining, shredding, storing and discovering documents and written testimonial from all the family paraphernalia stored over the years. And maybe this will help me discover who I am in the greater scheme of things. Or maybe it's all been just a totally traumatising distraction. I'll have to wait and see.

Elizabeth DeVita Raeburn writes that siblings are '...*signposts, of a sort, who help locate us in time and space, and in our families...*'. I'll buy that. And it is equally true that without them, we can feel so dislocated in time and space that all we can do is float and hope that something will moor us somehow, so we don't completely float away in to space.

Bette

Fuck 'em if they can't take a joke!

Bette Midler

The 8th of August 2017

Unlike any other icon, diva or celebrity, Bette Midler was the only one that had my brother and I, fuelled by crazy adoration and levels of euphoria that could launch a nuke, jetting from London, to NYC to Vegas and then back to London again. She was our shared experience, our guilty pleasure and the force of nature that defined and elevated a truly divine part of our lives in the years before Stewart died. She featured in his life and she certainly featured in his death. She will never know it, but The Divine Miss M was as much a part of the funeral, the memorial and the celebration of life as any of us for one simple, fabulous reason. We both love her.

The part she played in those rituals is already the stuff of record. But today, as I find myself YouTube flicking and clicking, my multimedia travels bring me back to clips from the shows we attended - *Kiss My Brass* at Radio City, *The Showgirl Must Go On* at Caesar's Palace and the most prized and treasured of all, *Divine Intervention* at The O2 in 2015, my 50th birthday gift to Stewart. I may have watched them time and time again but now they're rendered new and unfamiliar, triggering memories that thrill but that also land with a sadness and a punch in the gut that I'm guessing is just another part of all of this. Like ol' man river, it just keeps rollin' along.

But the divine Miss M had not only loomed large in our collective journey. She had first come to my attention in the months prior to another shocking event in my life; my father's sudden and unexpected death from a 'one night only' heart attack at the age of 52 in July of 1980.

In the eighteen months leading up to the night he died, during a period of tumult, secrets and lies (by this time, the things our family did best), I found myself drowning in drama and self-harming to the point of hospitalisation. No longer allowed access to the family home, I was exiled by my mother. But it proved a fortuitous banishment, because my father, himself long since exiled for his philandering ways, took me in. This was an act of kindness I never forgot, unexpected as it was, and which presented an opportunity to us both – the chance to meet for real for the first time. After all, we were seen as the damaged goods, the family's dirty secrets.

And it was one Saturday evening in the Autumn of 1978 that my father and I first met Bette Midler. Sitting together in the living room of his partner's home, watching *The Bruce Forsyth Show* – a family staple back in the late 70's – it was a pretty average weekend, except I was sitting there with a face full of stitches from a cutting episode that nearly went horribly wrong (or right depending on your perspective). Suddenly, following a suitably fabulous introduction, this crazy, manic Tasmanian devil of a diva appeared on the screen, all tight Lycra, corset and frizz perm and the screen almost exploded. Despite feeling that life was a lousy thing and I had no place in it, I looked up, perked up and sat up. My father appeared to do the same. We bonded over Bette. That evening she came into my life and she never left.

How it came to pass I never quite worked out – maybe I just didn't care – but within a few months my parents had convened a meeting behind closed doors (if this sounds political then that's because it just felt that way) and father was allowed to return. It felt weird and wrong. But what I recall with enormous fondness were the evenings when the two of us sat together alone, listening to the *Bette Midler: Live at Last* double album (ah, vinyl, how I love you still) just drinking in those funky 70's arrangements, wild and unleashed diva vocals and filthy, filthy Soph jokes that had us both laughing like loons, no matter how often we heard them. One year later, he was found dead in the back of his car in a wood near the Malvern Hills.

But it was almost as if that was just the scene-setter for Stewart and me. How and when my brother was first touched by the divinity of Ms. Midler, I frankly couldn't say. All I knew as I sat in front of my computer in 2004, poised, anxious and sweating to be the first in line when those Radio City tickets went on sale, was that I wanted my brother with me at the concert even if I had to pay for his ticket myself. Which I did.

And so, the rest really is history, wonderful, wistful and cherished history. It's the story of Stewart, Stephen & the Divine Miss M. She has been a constant through every peak, trough, crash, burn and bounce-back of our lives. And she was there when I needed her the most, singing soulfully as my brother made his final journey and then thereafter to belt it out in celebration of his life. And with great confidence and oodles of love, there is one thing of which I'm sure. If Stewart could tell you anything, Ms Midler, he would thank you from the bottom of his heart for all the 'hits, tits and glitz' served up during so many of his fifty-two years. And I can just imagine him walking up to you and, quoting that notorious alter ego Soph, look you in the eye and say with no small measure of joy, appreciation and gratitude, *I had a hell of a time. And I will never forget it*

Circle

When a sibling dies, we become different. But it doesn't show right away. It's the phantom limb sensation-a sense of both absence and presence.

Elizabeth DeVita Raeburn
The Empty Room: Understanding Sibling Loss

The 11th of August 2017: 11.20pm

One year ago, almost to the second, I arrived in Bournemouth to be met at the station by my brother and his partner, spending what would be my one and only weekend with him in his new apartment. Freshly purchased and newly adorned, here I was in Stewart-land, an adorable and totally muddled collection of mismatching furniture, randomly arranged in a gorgeous big living room with a lush bay window. I would have expected nothing less. One year on, and this is what I think about as it all buzzes around my brain like bees.

It was hot back then and I can almost conjure that feeling of heat as I write. A real scorcher, it was one of those special times together; relaxed, chilled and, as I think of it, an affirmation of how far we had come over the years. We couldn't have mattered more to one another it we tried. And at this point, we just didn't have to try.

But today, far from comforting, this anniversary of my visit – arranged originally to coincide with my upcoming birthday – kind of chews me up and spits me out. With a slap and a shove, my grief gremlin slips out of the shadows to remind me that my brother had gone, not on a trip but for good. Again, my breathing becomes erratic and so cue my little chest patting procedure.

In the book *Living with Grief after Sudden Loss*, Stephen P. Hersh draws attention to the fact that sudden loss of all kinds – heart attack, stroke, accident, homicide – can be equally as traumatic and devastating in many ways for all those left in its wake. Again, no comfort but at least it explains the recurrent judders, body-shocks and twitches that I have endured. These have increased in the weeks leading up to my birthday week. I remain almost pathologically knackered and I'm hyper-alert to the emotional knock-backs. When I spoke with Roger earlier this week, he caught me in a moment of relapse and so of course knew I was faking it as I attempted to be upbeat and peppy. His retreat into silence said it all. I felt he deserved an update. 'Roger, things haven't changed so don't worry. I just don't call everyone to state the obvious every time' I said. He was sorry he was not here to give me a hug and I replied 'I know' because I did. 'It's business as usual in this neck of the woods' I continued 'I just don't need to drag everyone into it as much'. This was not strictly true. I just believe my friends deserve a break from me and my grief.

Next weekend, I travel to Bournemouth and nothing will be as it was a year ago. No fun photos, no coffee and cake at *Flirt* cafe, no dinner for four and meeting new friends, no sitting around, acting up, bitching or joking. In short, no Stewart.

Instead, I will walk in to his flat and continue to pack and fold and sort. I will open the hospital bag that has been sitting there for over four months and then, in the company of little Steve, I will hold the last clothes my brother ever wore. And I need to prepare myself for whatever comes next. And I really have no idea what that might be. Rituals within rituals within rituals. Will they never end?

Stroke

Grief is an artist of powers as various as the instruments upon which he plays his dirges for the dead, evoking from some the sharpest, shrillest notes, from others the low, grave chords that throb recurrent like the slow beating of a distant drum.

Ambrose Bierce *The Boarded Window*

The 15th of August 2017

It occurs to me at this time every year - and that should come as no surprise to anyone - that forty-two years ago today, I had a stroke. Or a stroke-like thing. Or a TIA. Or whatever. Almost to the minute. It was mind-boggling because I was so young and made even more memorable by the fact that it happened the night before my 16th birthday. *Not-so-sweet sixteen.* And because it was my first startling encounter with my own mortality – a confrontation that had always led me to believe that I would surely be the first of three brothers to die – I think of both the episode itself, what it has meant to me over the years and most pointedly and poignantly what it means to me now, in the light of Stewart's death.

Timely then, that today I returned to my doctor to see if blood tests, casually encouraged in the shadow of my brother's passing, revealed any cause for concern. It was unlikely that they would. It was GP lip service, a placatory gesture in the event of sudden, unexpected death. Would it reveal if I too had inherited the congenital, hereditary condition that whisked Stewart away in the last, desperate beat of his heart? No, it would not. Lip service.

'So, what can we do for you today?' were the first words the GP spoke. Great start, I thought, you have no clue, or you've forgotten. I wanted to harm him, slam his head into the PC screen or stab him in the neck with the pen he kept clicking. Fucking arsehole, I thought, but he would never have known. 'The blood tests' I prompted politely 'in the light of my brother's sudden death in April'. He remembered. He reeled off some data, shared some percentages and ratios – yes, I have been reduced to a ratio – and talked about statins. He asked if I wanted some, told me that they could reduce cholesterol but beware, they had down sides including serious muscle pain and discomfort. 'Is there a problem with my cholesterol?' I enquired. He checked the file 'No, not really, it's a pretty average count and mainly good cholesterol'. I was confused but sat with it. He went on 'I'd like to do some more tests for haemoglobin. Do you smoke?' And for about the fiftieth time, I told him 'No'.

'Make another appointment when you leave' he ordered 'You may have just been dehydrated on the day, but we'll take another look anyway. Nothing to worry about'. Doctors really should avoid the phrase 'nothing to worry about' for obvious reasons.

I was in a funk for the rest of the day. Unsettled and lacking focus, I found comfort in my work. My bereaved client, attending for the first time since her mother's funeral, looked grey, exhausted and unwell. I know that look, I thought, the adrenalin tank has run dry. Lost in loss, she barely spoke. So, we sat with her harrowing, terrible pain and longing with occasional bursts of narrative where she told me about the day of her mother's cremation. How utterly, utterly unbearable, I thought.

Work attended to, I go back to unsettled, flicking through hundreds of online pages of rugs as I focus on the revamp of my consulting room. After rug 196, I feel all rugged-out and I know I must go to my bench on the heath. So, as is oft the way with the bench journey, I quickly become a man on a mission, grabbing my phone, earphones and bag as I hastily exit the apartment and head for my seat on high.

I walk along, wrapping my eyes in sunshades and securing my headphones. I flick through Spotify. And there's Barbra. Perfect. I walk onto the heath and into the sun. And there in the distance, barely visible through the early evening sunny blaze, sits that little rusting bench, a lump of old forged metal now dripping with memory and sadness. And in time, on my travels today, Streisand's *The Way We Were* strikes up, starting with that classic simple piano, followed closely by the unique Barbra hum. And there, in my recall, is Stewart, singing those very words on the big screen at his Celebration of Life, dreamily and perfectly in tune (unlike me during a tenure at Pontins holiday camp at age nineteen, when, for some reason I sang that very same song to a packed bar but, sadly, not in the same key as the band). As his female alter-ego, Lorelei, he sang this iconic Bergman-penned ballad at one of his cabaret events in Bournemouth, so the song now carries a particularly melancholic quality for me, both heart-breaking and soul-lifting at the same confusing time. So, I spend a little time back there at the Celebration, along with sixty special guests, frozen in time and watching the specially prepared film clip of Miss Lorelei, in one of her final shows singing about memory, love, loss and longing.

I take the path to the highest point on the heath and simply stand there. I'm not one for headphones and playlists but somehow, I am today. There is no-one around, other than dog walkers in the distance and way off, sportsmen warming up for rugby. So it's just me, the sun, the breeze and Barbra. It's indulgent, sentimental and evocative but no less real and true for that.

This is my first birthday without my brother on the planet and so no card dropping on the mat for me. He never forgot to send a card. No more cards.

Revelations

If you are bereft, accept that you have to trudge through each day as it comes, thankful when it is over and hoping for nothing better the next day or the day after.

(Mary Stott)

Virginia Ironside *You'll Get Over It: The Rage of Bereavement*

The 19th of August 2017

Bournemouth: The morning begins sunny enough but dark clouds threaten and there is a windy blustering that would usually forecast autumn but Summer has been a cyclothymic season this year so it should come as little surprise. Like me, it has been all over the place. I begin the day early and spend time alone unpacking the big hallway cupboard, installed at Stewart's behest, shortly after he moved in. Far better, he would think, to create more storage than throw out a single ball of Blu Tack or pot of drawing pins.

I press on and push through and by the time little Steve arrives, I feel child-like and in need of coddling and cradling. We hug with vigour, a strength that somehow speaks of the unenviable task at hand, although it is unlikely that any amount of holding and warm embraces will make this any less dreadful. So here we are, and it is time to open the hospital bag, containing the clothes in which my brother died. 'Shall we just get on and do it?' I ask. 'Sure' says little Steve 'whenever you want to'

I say 'I can't even remember where it is' as we walk to the bedroom but obviously I can. Maybe I also hope that someone has taken it or that it was never real in the first place. But it was and there it is. It sits in the dark corner, next to packing boxes and Stewart's laundry basket, also full of clothes from the last week of his life. I then reach for the bag and place it gently upon one of the already-full cardboard crates, where I open it cautiously. I lift out the first item; Stewart's thick wool Next coat. I hold it and picture him wrapped up in the cosy, woollen fabric that sunny but chilly April day. Organised, with files prepped for a training day and packed lunch in order, he would have made his way to the car park, placed bags in the back, started the engine and, with Bette belting out, he would have made his way along that familiar stretch of road – the A35 - to the hospice in Dorchester.

I continue and we both stay silent, almost as if we are just abiding by the formal protocol attached to the process of un-bagging the clothes of the deceased. I lift out trousers and a shirt and as they unroll, a pair of briefs and socks tumble out. None of the items have been folded and so lie in my hands, wrinkled and creased. Stewart would be furious. I imagine him choosing these for the last ever workday ahead. As he was running a workshop for volunteers, this garb would be my brother in 'trainer' mode so black dress trousers and posh slip-on shoes. No jeans or chinos today. He would have carefully made his selection.

And then there's the shirt. Almost the first thing I see is the stiffness in the material around the shoulders and neck where his blood dried over four months ago. This is what happened when he died, I thought. He bled. But why is it all over the place, I wonder, and then the narrative that I thought I knew changes with a tremulous shift. Having not been there, my fantasy had always been brutal but clean. Now that has been ripped from me. The scene is now violent and bloody. 'I wondered about blood' I say cryptically as I continue to inspect the shirt.

New images, new scenes, same outcome. There is blood in patches all over the shirt. Now my tragic scenario is also a bloody one. Friends and colleagues with blood on their hands and staining their clothes. Blood on the floor and all over Stewart's face. *A little bit of blood goes a long way.* Now I sense the panic, the pain, the urgency as attempts at resuscitation fail and he remains unconscious and bleeding. Maybe there were screams and shouting. I'll never know. I actually don't want to. But I'm holding my brother's dried blood in my hands and that I do know. I rub it and I have some crazy and distraught craving to press my face into the dried gore as if that will bring me close to him again. Staring at the black-red smears, I am dumb-founded, and I have no reference point for what I'm feeling.

And let's not leave out the fact that I am inconsolable as I weather all of this, crying so much that my tears get all mixed in with the blood and it reminds me of the chapel. Tears falling on cold, blue stars. But like then, I don't flail, wail or scream. I just cry. I cry until all the breath has left my body. And as I enter the zone, Steve rests his hand, gently, quietly on my back, before I partially slump into his shoulder. Silence.

It is some time before either of us can continue. I wonder what it must be like for him, coming face to face with Stewart's blood, dried into black patches all over the last shirt he ever wore. I don't even remember if I asked. I feel selfish and ashamed that it did not occur to me to ask. But I have no reason to suspect he feels that towards me at all.

The day is to be a long one with Viv joining us shortly to be part of the charity shop convoy as Stewart's belongings are ferried off to another life. So I fold back up all the creased/bloodied clothes, much as I had done with his entire wardrobe last month, return them to a new bag and place them on the highest shelf of the bookcase, knowing that I already have a plan for them. They will be cremated at a time yet to be decided but at least I have a plan. That provides a comfort of sorts. Sort of.

This is, I imagine, the only part of my journal that I will pen in Stewart's flat. As I tap away, the bag of bloodied clothes sits behind me, while the writing table sits in the centre of the room, illuminated by my brother's favourite pink-shaded floor lamp. And not to be ignored or discarded, Miss Lorelei (or her wig-blocked hair at least) peeps over my shoulder from the fireplace to my right, just keeping her eye on everything. So, for a few beats, I am still, a little less crazed than usual and maintaining the holding pattern. And in a moment – and it needs to be just a moment – it will be time to leave because staying in this almost-empty room for any longer might just be pushing my luck.

Shadow

Grief and sorrow are as unique to each individual as his or her fingerprints.

Lynda Chendelin Fell, Donna R. Gore & Nicola Belisle
Grief Diaries: Surviving Loss by Homicide

The 21st of August 2017

Today marks the anniversary of another significant death; Jenna's mother.

Just one year after my mother's death (January 1996), Jenna's mother, still young, succumbed to cancer and another violent cosmic rip appeared in someone's universe. And from my brother's flat, as I scooped up even more of his belongings prior to my journey home, we spoke by phone and she shared with me her plan for the day, a reflective, solitary moment of remembrance with time spent at the cemetery in Newmarket, significant simply because it was not how Jenna would usually mark the moment. We know that our mothers are everywhere and not confined to any final 'resting place'. We carry them always and everywhere. They pop up here and there, we sense them at our side, they sit on the side-lines of our lives, never too far away.

But another friend's encounter with death came to my attention shortly after my return to Royston. Far be it from Jenna and I to sanctify our mothers. They could be real pieces of work. They were flawed and fucked up like the rest of us and there are certain episodes of spectacular maternal failure that can still rock me to my core. Despite all things however, there is and will always be love. But sometimes, for some, there is instead unspeakable horror.

I had arrived home just minutes before when I heard the phone ring. I was memory box-ing in the attic and missed the call but, thinking it may be Jenna, I quickly descended the ladder and registered some surprise when I saw that the caller had been an old school friend, Helen. My surprise turned to curiosity due to the fact that she never calls, and I only usually call her when I'm planning a trip back to the Midlands and we meet for lunch. However, I returned the call immediately and I knew the moment I heard her voice that something was off.

After an awkward apology, almost as if she were apologising to her therapist for placing an out-of-hours call, she told me her story and therein lay the horror. One week ago, her mother had been found murdered. Worse, the guilty party had allegedly been a family member who, having killed her some time before the discovery of the body, had left her decomposing in her bedroom. I restrained myself because along with shock and concern for Helen, I was also intensely morbidly curious.

Helen was estranged from her mother, described her as 'a bitch to everyone' and confessed that in some way she was unsurprised that this woman had finally 'goaded' someone into killing her. I offered practical help and emotional support for whenever she wished to call. She thanked me and could not understand why she had suddenly become tearful that day. After all, her mother was a monster, she told me, so why should she cry for a monster? 'Grief is about many things' I shared, sounding a bit too therapist-y in my own head, 'You might feel a lot over time that makes no sense bearing in mind how things were with mum'.

Silence.

Then she said, 'Nobody wants to bury her. Everyone is just really angry and wants to walk away. My sister's fuming'

'Do you have anyone to talk to? Who's there for you, Helen?' I asked this because when assessing clients for the first time, I always have increased concern for those who do not feel they have a support system.

We spoke for about an hour. I listened, I offered some suggestions and I reacted as little as I could to the ghastly, gory details of it all. Body parts, autopsies, mouth swabs, decomposition, fluids and gore. Despite the bloody shirt at my brother's flat this was a whole new horror ball game. This is the rage/hate/murder version. It literally sounds like hell on earth. And my friend has just been relocated there.

Seasons

If you don't know how to die, don't worry; Nature will tell you what to do on the spot, fully and adequately. She will do this job perfectly for you; don't bother your head about it

Michel de Montaigne - French Philosopher

The 26th of August

Next week it will be September, which means Autumn. My consulting room has been face-lifted, revamped and glamorized and some kind of change and reconfiguration has become a thing I always seem to do during the Summer months, a throwback to my years working at the university maybe, when a new academic year was about to come stampeding over the horizon. And I remember it well. It really was like a stampede as thousands of freshers from the four corners of the globe came thundering onto campus, as terrified as they were excited. Many were simply terrified. Inevitably, they somehow found their way to us in the counselling and well-being department for a little bit of magic that would make the pain go away. We did what we could minus the magic. It was often never enough.

But, as much as I do not miss that relentless, unstoppable machine, some quirky little patterns remain. I have prepared for my new 'term'. My room looks fabulous even if I don't and that may simply be the fall-out and aftershocks from this week of weeks; bloody clothes, murder and remembrance. Oh, and not to forget the odd 'dizzy spell' I experienced in my brother's flat on Monday. Or the brother of all dreams that very same night, a night of trippy visions and psychedelic imagery.

In this dream, set in no particular space at no particular time, I feel the presence of my brother. It's always an impossible thing to try to describe, the 'presence' of a person in a dream. It could be a shape, part of them or just a feeling but somehow you just know it represents them. Anyway, we are huddled together, talking and laughing, doing impressions and acting like teenagers. Then, as if to punctuate the punch line, he takes hold of my hand and as we laugh, he gently squeezes it. With that, I awaken, but here's the thing. I can still feel him squeezing my hand and I remember thinking *Stewart, whatever you do, please don't let go of my hand.* But then it is gone, not quickly if I recall but slowly. In seconds, I drift off again. Maybe in search of him? I don't know. That part is not clear.

And then there was the 'spell'. I always thought that 'dizzy spell' was an Alan Bennett-type description reserved for something that happened to the elderly. A turn of phrase that covered a multitude of turns, maladies and conditions, taking in every possibility from a hot flush to a stroke. I've experienced both so I've earned my badge of honour.

And my turn happened as I sat alone in Stewart's flat on Monday of this week, looking around a room now riven of all his novelties, fairy lights and knickknacks. I remember that one moment I was sitting, reflecting and remembering and the next, I could hardly focus, and everything was splitting and shifting from side to side, like a 60's psychedelic movie dream sequence. The decision to stand was perhaps not my finest moment but that is what I did. It was not long before I made the executive decision that I needed to be horizontal in my own best interest and, woozy headed, speedily lowered myself to the floor. So, I lay there and rolled to face the ceiling. And my eyes filled up and my face flushed red hot. Then, with a certain sense that I could be verging on hysteria, I started to laugh as I thought, if only for a moment *I hope there isn't a flat viewing any time soon.* Imagine some young and enthusiastic first-time buyer walking in on a prostrate grieving ageing homosexual having a 'turn' on the floor of a potential new home. Scarred for life.

But no-one came, I slowly gathered myself and I stood slowly, half expecting to blackout and hit the deck. And I remembered in that moment, my stroke episode alongside Stewart's shock departure and for a moment, as was to be expected, I wondered again if this was it. I wondered once again this year, with no sense of fear or emerging panic if I would, could die in Stewart's flat, just as my 'work' here was so almost over. 'Oh, don't be silly' some might say. 'You're just over-reacting' others might add, as another rush of fear and mortal dread gets projected on to me.

But there's a simple bottom line. Those sentiments, those flip judgements and reprimands would fall on deaf ears. It's hard to see my dark deliberations as disproportionate knee jerks when one has already fallen foul of a stroke-like thing at age fifteen and then more recently exposed to a traumatic hammering in the aftermath of a loved one's sudden death.

Phase

There is no magical anaesthetic for the pain of grief

Colin Murray Parkes *The Price of Love*

The 31st of August 2017

I have done a lot. But what when there is little left to do? I have used many words and phrases over the months – free-falling, lost, abandoned, unknown territory, space, foreign land, surrender – but this phase, or maybe evolution of a phase, has just become a kind of nothing *plus*, an extension of the limbo.

Last week, I had a Skype supervision session with my clinical supervisor, who was based that day in London, and I was unable to travel to see him in person.

'You look grey' he told me. I wish I could have blamed the lighting, but I knew what he meant. Grief and its cohort can do that to a person. It is the very same word I used to describe my client the previous week, deep in the throes of her post-funeral collapse. Grey.

As we concluded, he mentioned therapy, as in, 'Have you considered going back into therapy?' I nodded heavily and said yes.

So, who will I choose, we wonder? The search begins with this conversation I suppose but I'm not about to just pull a name out of a hat. But I do need to be on the case and *stay* on my case or the case may indeed go cold. And then I need to start from the beginning – and we're back at the morning of the 6th of April 2017. On one level, it's a dreadfully unappealing prospect.

Now it's an understatement to say that I have had a lot of therapy over the years and I've been working with clients since 2003 and, with that in mind, I wonder who would be up to the job. But that pompous line of enquiry is just a good old fear defence mechanism, the classic aversion tactic. Which is all very psychobabble-y but it's a defence that may not serve me in the long term, and so the search begins. The fact that I don't want to go leads me to believe I absolutely need to. As they say, therapy is like comedy. It's all in the timing.

Therapy

You're not crazy. You're grieving.

Megan Devine *It's OK That You're Not OK*

The 1st of September 2017

In my ongoing disturbed, fidgety state, distracting myself with this, that and the other, I have entered a sort of deep freeze, indolent and listless. Colour drained away, I am back to wondering what the point of it all is, while also not really caring much anyway. It's what I imagine one of the seven circles of hell might be like.

So, it's time then. I imagine it will feel odd, disorienting even. Time to be a client again. I'm suddenly compelled to hear me tell my own story and I need to hear it all tumble out of my mouth without having to consider how it will sound or what shape/form it might take. All sharing up to this point has been with the involved and invested but that chapter is now a done deal. There are no more baubles to hand out, mementos to share or strings of fairy lights to distribute so friends can light up their homes with a little bit of Stewart. It's done. That little bijoux flat on the coast is all but empty, but for a bag of bloody clothes and I'll get to them soon enough.

Jolt

Grief no more needs a solution than love needs a solution. We cannot 'triumph' over death, or loss, or grief. They are immovable elements of being alive.

Megan Devine *It's OK That You're Not OK*

The 2nd of September 2017

I think when someone you love dies, there is at least one other death of sorts - you. You lose who you were. Not for all time and not in all ways but the person you were with that person beside you in the world no longer exists. Your internal system, relationally, emotionally and spiritually, needs to reconfigure, re-frame and reintegrate around the grief and loss. Oh, where to begin?

It is a well-known and well-worn consideration in the grief-work field that part of this ghastly long day's journey is the gruelling endeavour to find yourself again in the world, or should I say the world that you have known. The view from here loses shape and form, textures are flattened and the colour drains from the everyday. In other words, disintegration, desolation and depression stretches as far as the eye can see. You constantly flash back only to ricochet forward again, forgetting for a moment, not so much where you just went but where you are now. The kaleidoscopic muddle corrects itself in a second, but it still feels like something's messing with your mind.

At times, there is comfort too. And safety if you can find the energy, motivation and drive to seek it out. Today, I travelled into London to spend time with Roger where I wobbled for a second when we met and then found my feet some moments later so our day could continue. It was a simple and familiar time spent together, involving, as usual, copious amounts of coffee, brunch at Balans restaurant and ice cream. There *has* to be ice cream.

But what reassured me that things may not be as relentlessly doom-laden as they feel was the spring that developed in my step, the zing from the strings of my heart and the lift I received as we turned the corner off the Strand and finally, after months of promise and prevarication, bought our tickets FINALLY for the musical, *Dreamgirls*. 'We're your Dreamgirls, boys' they sing 'We'll make you happy'. They better.

And as the old mantra goes; while there's musical theatre, there's hope.

Fugue

*While grief is fresh, every attempt to divert only irritates. You must
wait till it be digested*

Samuel Johnson (Poet)

The 4th of September 2017

Oh, to find myself subjected to a fugue state. Not for ever maybe but just
a fugue state vacation or interlude or intermission. OK, I'll settle for a long
weekend but anything to achieve some respite from this ever-escalating,
never ending smack, bang, wallop.

So as we enter Autumn and I wear my grief like dirty old clothes that
have fused to my skin and as neighbours and fellow flat owners in the court
sell up to move on and the inevitable rogues gallery of transient tenants
descend upon the place to wreak havoc (it'll happen, mark my words), I
crave travel, a journey, to be whisked away. Where to is anyone's guess but
anywhere will do. Which got me to thinking: What would it actually be
like to be in a fugue state?

A fugue state is a psychiatric condition which finds a person at the mercy
of a compulsion to travel and wander alongside of which emerges a new
identity. This is not some witness protection type thing, you understand.
This is a condition that renders the sufferer helpless, utterly at the mercy of
this spooky and bizarre dissociative state. Sounds like heaven.

Who would I be? What would that new identity look like? Would I
be male or female? Where would I end up and what dark and troubled
unconscious process would influence my 'wanderings'? But it really must
come to something when a condition so extreme sounds like time out. But
it does and I'm probably desperate and giving it a glamorous spin, desperate

to know what life feels like minus the experience of being pilloried night and day by grief gremlins and the hordes of memory that smother me in my sleep. *Stewart, where have you gone?*

But fugue states are not known to last and memories and identity soon return thereafter. Damn! I knew it sounded too good to be true. Oh well, back to the drawing board.

So, in the meantime, I write, drink red wine and listen to Bette; songs about seasons and weather, about the power of all kinds of love and songs about grief and loss.

And as we get older, even Ms. Midler acknowledges that lyrics that were once about relationships are now about loss, ballads that on one level spoke of lovers now just speak of friendship, chosen family and the stuff of being human. I was really affected by her reappraisal of *Stay With Me* at the O2 concert, which thirty five years ago spoke to tortured love and bleeding hearts but now as we all age and move towards final curtains of one kind or another, becomes a cry of loss, grief and mourning. Her mid-song spoken bridge now goes like this -

I never knew that so many people that I knew and love would become ghosts to me. They're memories hovering over me like a misty cloud. And I guess there's a little bit of rage in there too, ya know. Why did you leave me behind? Why did you leave me behind??

Stewart and I sat just ten rows from Bette as she performed her reinterpretation. I recall so vividly how I felt. I was whisked away somewhere as she spoke of ghosts and mist and rage. Who knew it would come back to me now as if to drive the point home?

So maybe I'll take a pass on the fugue state. It sounds way too disturbing anyhow. Grief rips you apart but at least you know where you stand, albeit barely. And I certainly know where I stand with my own ghosts, mist and rage. Would I really want it to be any different? To wander off into a new identity would be to lose the only thing I can be sure of at the moment.

Bath

She has invented a new relationship with him, one that acknowledges that he is dead, gone from her life but present, too

Elizabeth DeVita-Raeburn on 'Meredith'
The Empty Room: Understanding Sibling Loss

The 6th of September

Today, I take the train from Paddington to Bath, treasured cargo – my brother's remaining ashes – carefully placed in a small black, velvet purse and sealed inside my brown leather shoulder bag. No, that's not accurate. It is, in fact, Stewart's bag and I have adopted it.

I have arranged to meet with someone called Jamie at *Bath Aqua Glass* where I will hand him the remains. He will then do whatever glass artists need to do to accurately determine how many memorial orbs can be created from these little particles of Stewart. 'I don't want any left over' I shall say. Immortalized forever, these orbs certainly have what it takes to last until the end of days. Oh, I forgot to mention; these are not for me. They are gifts of gratitude for the bereaved collective on Stewart's side of things. I don't plan to force them on anyone because no-one should ever feel obliged to accept anything made from a dead person, wouldn't you agree?

The train leaves on time and I should be in Bath just before 3pm which is my ETA at the glass works. But there are long delays *en route* and I have extra time to read, drink coffee and every now and then, take the black velvet bag from my case and hold it in my hand. That's all I do. I hold it, look at it, feel something and then return it to the inside pouch. For a moment, I let myself wonder which bit of Stewart the ash represents. I'll never know but I wonder, nonetheless.

I read *The Empty Room* by Elizabeth DeVita-Raeburn. It has been a comfort blanket for some weeks now and the chapter I read on this trip presses buttons and flicks switches and all of a sudden, I am excited by what I read. After all these weeks of wondering how I can sort of maintain contact with my brother and at the same time live a rich, full existence in my own right, I'm presented with the key. And here, in DeVita-Raeburn's book, it's called 'carrying'.

I cannot read it fast enough. Why this all comes as news to me only now doesn't really matter. After all, it is really just a very accessible re-framing of Dennis Klass and Phyllis R. Silverman's Continuing Bonds Theory, which flips 'get over it' beliefs on their head and kicks them to the curb. In short, it encourages the bereaved to move towards a new and transformed relationship with those who have died, while never forgetting that they have physically gone. This takes many different shapes and forms. It does not deny the pain, but it offers something to place alongside it. It offers choice and possibility and hope, not for the dead to return or rise up but to become something else.

As the train finally crawled back into motion towards Bath, I happened upon a memory from the day my brother died and I remember saying, as I ricocheted around in shock and bewilderment, 'I'll just have to find a new way to have a relationship with him'. It feels like a really mystifying, freaky thing to have said in a way but I will, and I have and I shall continue to do so. Because this orb mission is just one example of many and I have made the choice to do it, this carrying thing, along with all the other siblings in the world who have lost brothers and sisters they love and long for. Elizabeth DeVita Raeburn puts it best when she says -

How people try to do so may vary, but why we do it is more straightforward. We try to carry our siblings forward because they are part of our identities, and our half of the relationship doesn't end with their deaths. We need them as reference points to remember who we are

Attic

*And can it be that in a world so full and busy the loss of one creature
makes a void so wide and deep that nothing but the width and depth
of eternity can fill it up!*

Charles Dickens *Dombey & Son*

The 7th of September.

The dizzy spell experience at Stewart's flat some weeks ago was, as it
happens, no fluke or one-off. This evening, while shopping in Morrisons,
the split-screen, wobbly vision, cross-eyed combo was upon me again. I
thought it was a moment in time but apparently not. Fearing that I was
about to keel over by the frozen desserts, I latched onto a shelf, grateful and
relieved that no-one was around. About a minute later it had passed. And
yet I knew the genesis of this thing. I just knew. As you do.

But at least I did not faint. I reined in the anxiety even though the hot
flush and sweat all over was something beyond my control and I continued
on my way. Back home, I started to get the shakes but not too badly.
Maybe this was just a panic response. I certainly know what those feel like
by now. And maybe next week's blood tests will reveal the haemoglobin
issue was not a mere aberration and I will get a diagnosis of something like
anaemia that provides an answer. Or maybe I'm just shooting in the dark,
clutching at straws and all that jazz. We'll see.

And then came the familiar (but not so regular these days) thump in the
chest. That throat tightening, almost retching feeling of craving, longing
for my brother to be live and in person on planet earth. I did not feel
inclined to reach for the comfort of memory, I did not want the immediate
connection I feel when I place my hands on the orb. I wanted my brother

back. This feels like grief cold-turkey again and the only antidote is Stewart back in my world. My dark passenger is there to kick me back to the reality of my loss.

In a flash of something like animal instinct, I knew where I wanted to be. I took hold of the long crank key, raised it to the attic hatch and inserted it into the catch. One twist and it released, the flap dropping down slightly so that the crank handle, doubling as a hook, could latch onto it and pull it down. I unfolded the ladder and made my way up into the roof. It was dark and yet with one flick of a switch, the big colourful string of lights that coursed down the side of the space and then wrapped around Stewart's memory box jumped flamboyantly to life.

I have a large, stand-up attic stretching the length of the living room. Before my brother died, this was just a spartan space of v-shaped rafters and a simple floor that I had installed when I moved in some four years ago. Now, it is consecrated ground, a hallowed place and another space to visit that might offer a vestige of comfort. Might.

I follow the illuminated string – large, multi-coloured glowing spheres, more like circus tent adornments than fairy lights – and I kneel, still a little dizzy, by the memory box. Mine sits close by but I pay it no mind. That will eventually come to mean something to someone but not so much to me. I reach out and place my hand gently upon the top and yes, I do indeed feel some kind of solace, as the giddiness fades to black.

Flash, flash, flash. There it goes again. Images from both when Stewart was alive and after he had died. The flashes continue as I lay down upon my side. I pull myself into a consoling foetal position. My hand is still resting on the lid and this too calms me in the semi-darkness of this cobwebby place with only a strand of circus lights for company.

I could have lay there for hours but I did not. I remember singing a bit - this may be a gay brother/West End Wendy/grief thing, but I think it was a muffled, mad version of Liza Minnelli's *And the World Goes Round* which seemed apt. And if this all really does sound a bit mad, then good. Job done. Because that's also how it felt.

Clearing

You have no power over the death but you do have power over the story

Virginia Ironside *You'll Get Over It: The Rage of Bereavement*

The 14th of September 2017

It is something like entering a clearing in the woods, with the knowledge that you will inevitably have to journey deeper into that unknown and spooky copse while for a moment bestowed with a little light. And allowed to breathe a little freer in air a little fresher, even if only briefly.

It's just now since arriving in the 'clearing' that I rain-check the past three weeks and realise that I have really struggled. No, I mean *really* struggled. And at the same time, it's something of a paradox – I feel temporarily released from something and at the same time miss my brother even more intensely. Memories go 'boo!' and set me spinning and I guess they always will. How do I know this? Because I want them to and I recall the words that one of the contributors, H.D.Kirkpatrick wrote about his own brother, recorded in the text *Sibling Loss Across The Life Span*, when he simply states that *'...there is a loving grief that keeps my brother alive...'*. I like his idea of 'loving with grief' because as he goes on to say, *'loving grief never ends'*. Nonetheless, currently, I gasp a little, weep a lot and lie in a heap. I think; Shall I spend some time with the memory box, the circus lights and the cold of the attic? No, not now, I decide, but I'm sure I will. Loving grief never ends.

Just a few days ago, on her return from Burning Man, Heather met up with me in London for a Sunday brunch affair to talk about the life-changing craziness of the annual Nevada festival, to gladly accept my request to co-execute my will and, out of the blue, to set in motion the table read for my play *Big Bad Trouble*, which feels like it's been 'in development' longer than it took to make *Boyhood*. Now, this epic trash romp has been written, re-written, re-formatted and reimagined more times since its bizarre inception in 2003 than a Trump executive order but we got here in the end. Heather's enthusiasm to be involved not only shows great courage (she was deeply involved with the semi-filmed version from 2008 which sent most of us mad, one of us spiralling into addiction and another seeking refuge in a field in France) but a real faith in the project. It's not a production but it's an essential next step.

But what makes Heather's presence and long-lasting special friendship so very significant to me now is not only how long we have known each other – it really is thirty years next year – but that she knew Stewart (albeit sketchily) through me for almost as long. She also offered unwavering support when our mother died in 1996. 'Do you want me to come?' I recall her asking me during a phone call back then when I was at my most incomprehensible. Then, knowing the answer, she simply added 'I'll come'. And she did, the next day driving from London to the Midlands to be with me that muddy, grey day in January 1996, when Stewart and I said our final funeral farewells to our mother. As we spoke of Stewart, we remembered this time too.

Whether it was this reunion, the emotion we both felt and the love that we share, I really have no idea but this day ended with another utterly bizarre night of weird dreams and nightmares where friends became foes, the twilight zone ate me and a cult descended upon Royston. But for all that, the next day, I entered the 'clearing'. My grief feels less cluttered, my pain not so abrasive and my brother's essence/spirit thing closer. I know he's gone but he is present. I feel hopeful in the clearing.

Search

So try to be patient and courageous: patient in leaving the problems unresolved for the time begin, and courageous in not giving up the struggle for their final solution.

Viktor Frankl *The Will to Meaning*

The 22nd of September 2017

All in all, what a year of death and destruction it has been. And as overwrought as it may sound – and let's face it, it's a pretty overwrought world currently – if we search amongst the wreckage and debris, we find other things. For every scream, there is an embrace, for every collapse, there can be someone ready to catch you when you fall and for every death, well, that will bring out the best in some and the worst (or nothing) in others. And I know all this is true.

Celebrated psychiatrist Viktor Frankl spoke of love in the shadow of the concentration camps. He wrote '*...love goes very far beyond the physical person of the beloved. It finds its deepest meaning in his spiritual being, his inner self. Whether or not he is actually present, whether or not he is still alive at all, ceases somehow to be of importance*'. Knowing Frankl's history has always made him the most extraordinary of public voices and I was drawn to his terrible narrative and his therapeutic paradigm – that of logotherapy – early on in my training as a therapist. While his psychological philosophy was not borne directly of this horrific 'dark night' in his life, I cannot imagine that his time exposed to and suffering the horrors, the death and the depravity of the camps did not then profoundly colour the subsequent development of his model.

And without my brother in the world, I do know, as alone in the dark as I might feel, that my love for him not only survives but grows and becomes something else, something more. In other words, it transcends. Of course, another part of me says 'fuck that' with a scowl because my earthbound human self is still wrecked and wretched. No talk of spirit and transcendence can comfort that part. Time will or will not tell if these bits and pieces of me will ever come together, integrate, synthesise. I have no way of knowing. Simply, painfully put, I know that I don't know.

Empty

*We simply don't have the energy to dramatically grieve our way into a
state of healing and harmony*

Cheryl Eckl *in Psychology Today*

The 26th of September 2017

The second wave is not unlike the first, except only that it's not the first.

Despite carrying on regardless, pushing through, cancelling or
postponing very few of my plans, adding to the mix, dancing as fast as I
can, stepping out, going up and over, weeping, wailing and gnashing teeth,
there is one destination, one brutal rock bottom, that leaves me nowhere to
run, basically because I wouldn't have the energy anyway.

And I have arrived.

Burnout.

Shattered

The message was clear: it was futile to avoid my grief; I had to let it swallow me whole.

Lynda Cheldelin Fell & Christine Bastone
Grief Diaries: Surviving Loss of a Sibling

The 28th of September 2017

I don't think I believe that grief dissipates as it storms along. Rather, I believe it is like the storms we have witnessed ripping up entire islands in recent weeks. So much seems to be getting ripped up these days – islands, the world, trust, faith, hope, me. This is global grief and loss in the time of Trump.

So, going along with my weather allegory, I'll expand. I knew this past weekend that things were gathering momentum again, increasing to another category, when, meeting with friends, I learned surprisingly that the vaguest, slightest mention of my brother, caught in my chest like a hook. There again was the gasp, that halting, mini-shock of a gasp that has been stopping me in my tracks. Dining out, theatre trips and relaxing brunches in the West End are wonderfully therapeutic distractions but when that storm picks up and you are distracted no more, you just brace yourself and cling to anything that's bolted down. Currently, I am not bolted down.

Today, I saw six clients – which included two hours supervising senior management from the hospice. I remember wondering to myself 'Will I get through this?'. I remember a quote, source unknown - *'I'm so tired my soul hurts'*. That just about sums it up. But I get through it and somehow find the oomph to bring me home. No catastrophes in therapy world today thankfully.

But I lumber from one day's end to the next, shambling along, doing the do and going through the motions. And alone, I slump and plod and pant as if I'm ninety years old in the shade. No-one tells you about the spiritual fatigue, the draining debilitation that wrings out your soul in one fell swoop. This feels like the real danger zone of grief because there's no time off, vacation or distraction that recharges this energy source. I have to hold fast. Just that. Hold fast and sit with it. Because you can sleep as long as you like, yoga yourself into a knot and take cathartic, inspirational walks till your feet bleed but nothing can fend this off.

This isn't a stage, it's a threat. It tells you 'I will pass, when I pass'. And I ask, 'But what must I do to endure, to survive you?'. 'You will or you won't' it replies. Great fucking help. I was right. It's a threat.

If I could call out to my brother from this hot zone of trepidation and fear, I would ask him to help me but I'm so busy being battered and blinded by gale-force emotions, that I can't get a word in edgeways.

And for me to not get a word in edgeways, it must be bad. Just ask anyone.

Train

There is another kind of fury, a free-floating anger, turning the bereaved person into a loose cannon, surprising even himself with his random discharges of unfocused rage.

Virginia Ironside *You'll Get Over It: The Rage of Bereavement*

The 29th of September 2017

Today, I wouldn't want to meet me on a dark night. I'd love to hit someone. Just give me an excuse, I dare you. Bang me with your case, knock the back of my seat, get in my way or just keep jabbering at the bank counter when I'm waiting to be served. My fantasies are murderous, rageful and full of blood. I feel cruel, unlikable and ugly inside and out. It's been getting harder for me to be with me over the past two weeks but like Sarah Paulson's ambivalent conjoined twins in *American Horror Story: Freak Show*, I'm stuck with me.

I'm on a train to Bournemouth and I'm angry with my brother that I must endure this journey again. Of course, I don't have to but I'm not in my right mind these days, so I believe I do. But this weekend is different, I tell myself, because this is the final chapter – in other words, my brother's flat must be as empty when I leave on Monday as it was the day he first moved in. I watch the clock – 21.56, 21.57, 21.58. If I stare at those digital numbers much longer, I'll likely burn out my retinas, so I stop. And maybe I've got it wrong.

Maybe these journeys, these missions, these never-ending proceedings that I force-feed myself every month are no good for me whatsoever. Maybe – not easy to say, this – maybe I'm addicted. But this 'hit' is different because I'm a seething mass of resentment. Stewart, I'm so pissed off with you, I really am. You died and you left me and I have mourned you, I have paid tribute to you, I have shared with strangers how much I love you and I have celebrated you. Well, where's the How-Fucking-Dare-You ritual?! Can I have one of those please? A space to rage at you, to slag you off for doing this, to vent my spleen, to put you in the cross-hairs of my weeping, wailing anger and just scream 'Fuck you, fuck you, fuck you!'. Because I love you and you shouldn't be able to just die like that and leave me ripped inside out, guts everywhere. Like I say, not of sound mind.

So, I'm on the train and I'm looking around and I'm curious about how come so many morbidly obese people are in this carriage. I'm not judging, it's just an observation. Actually, that's a lie. I want to ask them 'How did this happen? And don't say it's hormonal or 'I don't eat that much' because that's just a lie. Jeez, step away from the crisps NOW!'. But there is a resentful mutated bit of grief that wonders simply 'Why are you alive and sitting there in all your lager-swilling, crisp-munching glory when my brother is dead. Sorry, what's that you're mumbling through a mouthful of crap??? Yeah, and fuck you too' Which is ripe coming from me, sitting here, overweight and eating chocolate covered toffee popcorn as I write. Oh well, I guess you're right. Fuck me too.

Time trots away and still, I'm on a train to Bournemouth. A busy week stretches behind me and I reflect on it all as the train leaves Winchester, the clock scrolls and I drink tea. Apparently, I'm inspirational or so a supervisee at the hospice told me earlier in the week. Bereavement becomes me. More reminders and little snapshots from the week – HIV, addiction, crystal meth, porn stars, end of life care, cancer, heart attack, death, mother. A pause. Stewart. Silence.

The train grinds to a sudden halt. As do I.

Done

There are still a lot of mournful moments. I continue to miss him, because there are constantly new things that I want him to be there for…It's been 12 years, but the loss is still fresh; I still grieve (Marion & Ted)

Maria Piantanida
The Oxidation of Grief: Reflections on Adult Sibling Loss

The 2nd of October 2017

I'm at the flat. Journey's end. Well, to this point at least. I think back over and recall all the weekends spent at my brother's flat since he died. And I can remember every last one of them and how the emotional colours and textures have changed over time. One thing, however, has been a constant. I have handled this whole labour of love and loss with kid gloves almost as if it were made of glass and could shatter, along with me, at any given moment. It's been intense but at least I can say with confidence that everything – well, nearly everything. The British Heart Foundation couriers were rude and paradoxically heartless - went to plan. Job done. Boxes ticked. Time to leave.

I'm on a train back to London Waterloo. I'm drinking red wine because I deserve it and I'm writing this because it's what I'm in the habit of doing. Eyes closed with a big sigh, I let my thoughts wander as I scroll back. Yesterday, shortly before leaving the flat, now stripped bare of all its idiosyncratic decor other than the floral print drapes, I sit alone in the dark and there too drank red wine. In the last, fading minutes of daylight, I kneel on the floor in the living room with that gorgeous high ceiling far above me, and I raise my glass. 'Stewart' I say 'I toast to you, to me, your friends and mine. To all of us. I hope we did you proud. I love you' And I drink as my face glows and my eyes begin to sting. 'I know so much more about you now than I did six months ago' I turn to look at all the papers, diaries, letters and photographs I have discovered, sifted through and appraised 'I know you better now than I did when you were alive'. I drink to that dark irony.

So, it's done. There is now no need at all for me to return to the flat except to clear odds and sods in the light of a sale completion date and that day is at least three months away. If I choose to return in the interim however, then that may be a sign that all is not well with me. I cannot imagine that happening however because, when all is said and done, this is one large, looming shadow that has finally faded to nothing.

Stewart

None of us…can stop another's trajectory toward death. But through our caring, even when less than perfect, we may help to alleviate the loneliness of the journey.

Maria Piantanida
The Oxidation of Grief: Reflections on Adult Sibling Loss

The 6th of October 2017

My dear Stewart, my beloved brother, six months ago to the day, you died. I am almost lost for words. I am almost lost full stop. If anyone had ever asked me 'What do you dread most in your life, in this world?', I would not have said this. Because that would have been to imagine it and I simply would not have been able to go there. It was unfathomable to me, utterly unimaginable and quite unbearable to consider or imagine a physical world without you. But, unfathomable or not, here I am. In a Stewart-less world. I have to find a way to tolerate the intolerable. No imagination required. This is real. You have gone away.

I looked towards this six-month marker as if to somehow make it meaningful, to give me something to aim towards. Next, I'll be doing the same with a year and doubtless putting some plan, plot or journey in place to raise you from the dead. Maybe I'll find myself at the burial site, talking to you in the ground and messing with the soil or standing on a cliff in Bournemouth, gazing longingly out to sea and dripping with sadness or sitting with friends being terribly eloquent about 'the gift of grief' and all that it has given me (although the latter is highly unlikely, bearing in mind my feelings about such platitudes). But, Stewart, as I sit here, as night falls, as the planet spins, all I remember is the futility, the gut-gouging, the prayer to the universe to let me die too, the cold flesh, the heavy bruise, your dead body, plastic pipes forced up your nose and down your throat and since that time six months ago, I also have the snapshot of bloodied clothes, the latest installation in my gallery of grief.

Stewart, you have been spared all this. That is some kind of perverse comfort, but I still pine and yearn. I'm not evolved or grown-up enough to rise from your ashes just yet. And Stewart, I think you would have been proud, as I am, that I have carried on (while never keeping calm), with devastation walking at one side and some kind of madness keeping pace on the other. And, with these constant companions in tow, it often feels as if my grip on reality is slowly but surely being prized away from the cliff face. The only reason I don't let it happen is because I fear something worse waits on the rocks below, like not dying.

Stewart, six months ago to the day you died. So why does it still feel like it just happened?

Threads

It would be nice if something made sense for a change

Lewis Carroll *Alice's Adventures in Wonderland*

The 7th of October 2017

With grief, there is a sense of being very loosely stitched together where, with one simple tug on an exposed thread, you would literally tumble into pieces. That is the feeling.

Stop

I know why we try to keep the dead alive: we try to keep them alive in order to keep them with us. I also know that if we are to live ourselves there comes a point at which we must relinquish the dead, let them go, keep them dead

Joan Didion *The Year of Magical Thinking*

The 12th of October 2017

I journey on. That is what I have been saying over the months when asked 'How are you?'. It really is the best I can do because beyond that, I don't really know much.

Thing is, I don't think I know how I am. I could say 'Well, I'm getting up in the morning' or 'I'm doing what needs to be done' or 'Getting by'. All contain a modicum of truth but really all I can attest to is that I am somehow in some way in motion.

Despite it all, it would be true to say I'm 'getting by'. But who the hell wants to just get by? Busier than I would be usually, my client base has grown significantly in recent weeks and yet I still, for some utterly, blindly deranged reason, schedule in training days for hospice staff on three consecutive Saturdays. They appear to be going really well. Hardly the point though where one is just 'getting by'.

With a new offer in on Stewart's flat – accepted after the lip-service back and forth negotiation – and that last weekend of clearance, a line is drawn and after six long months I now have no future plans to re-visit the coast. *It will be hard when you close that door for the last time*, others say. *Oddly, I don't think so*, I reply. There is more of my brother here now in Royston than remains back in Bournemouth. Photos, fairy-lights, cuddly toys, laundered clothing, his ashes suspended in glass, ornaments and a shirt covered in blood – they're all here.

But it all sure takes a toll and next week is my official well-being week. I begin therapy, I've booked a massage, I will continue the cardio classes and I expect to see the physio at some point, that is, if he is recovered sufficiently from his bowel cancer treatment to be back in business. I haven't spoken with him since the day before Stewart's death and a lot has happened and much has changed. I'm assuming at this point that he is still alive. But maybe not. I know better to assume anything these days.

Resuscitation

In the earliest days following loss, the thought that anything good can come from our experience is beyond comprehension. Yet some say there are blessings in everything.

Lynda Cheldelin Fell & Christine Bastone
Grief Diaries: Surviving Loss of a Sibling

The 17th of October 2017

Fitsteps is a cardio-based, strictly choreographed exercise programme. It is extremely fast, very sweaty and makes you feel old even if you're not. And I am. Like Norma Desmond, I have instigated, rather than a comeback, a return. I had given it up, following a pulled something-or-other and believed that I had really passed my Fitsteps sell-by date. Time to retire, I thought.

Then, at the height of my free fall into the bereavement abyss, I bumped into Tara, the teacher of the aforementioned class, in a local Tesco. We hugged and chatted, and I found myself encouraged back into the line of physical fire. So, I revved up for my return.

When I did, it was extraordinary, and I felt as if I were home. It literally felt like home and, at this time of times, I need to feel that home is somewhere. I don't need to know why or how it is that 45 minutes of non-stop latin and ballroom shenanigans takes me there. Maybe it had something to do with the familiar, the cathartic reminder that things go on or the sense of community. Anyway, it did the trick.

So, this has become part of my resuscitation protocol and slowly but surely, I have more than just soul-pummelling grief in my life. I also have the Paso-doble, the tango and the quick step.

Tomorrow, I add another building block and call up a therapist, recommended by my old supervisor. And it's been quite a time since I took to the client chair, let me tell you. I know the other chair so well. The comfortable chair. The professional chair. But this is that other chair. The scary, exposing, all-about-me chair. Imagining myself swapping seats is doing my head in a bit, to be frank. Do I even know how to be a client anymore? I guess I'll know by this time tomorrow. I'm cringing.

I live my life staring in to the dark, hard face of my brother's death. I have made self-soothing decisions and sometimes, as sure as night becomes day, some self-sabotaging ones to boot. *Sure, I'll run a training for your nursing staff on Saturday. What's that you say? They can't all come on the same day so could I do it three Saturdays in a row? Sure, why not. I'll even make tea, buy a projector, book the room and blow glitter out my arse.* Like I said, not always self-soothing. What on earth possessed me?

Heart

…death and loss often go together: for loss is of another person, and death is about oneself. Of the two, loss tends to be easier to talk about and therefore may be addressed in preference to – and to the exclusion of – the more difficult issue of death.

Mick Cooper & Martin Adams
Existential Perspectives on Human Issues

The 23rd of October 2017

In recent days, I couldn't be bothered to write. Just that. I could not bring myself to record anything or everything that I was doing, feeling and being. And that's a lot. But I have just picked up my trusty Chromebook and here we are.

My week off hardly felt like a week off at all and that's my fault. I sandwiched a Monday to Friday break between two working weekends, running those training workshops for hospice staff on both Saturdays and then fielding calls Monday to Friday from the insurance company, regarding follow-ups and new referrals. As a result, I'm now having a 'WTF???' moment as this sinks in. But there was at least time to meet with Jenna, witness Roger's return to the stage in a local production of the musical *Parade* (cheery little piece about child murder and wrongful convictions) and return once again to the client chair (yes, it was weird. Timely, but weird).

That client chair was waiting for me in Cambridge, away from the core of the city centre. On the day, my journey on foot from the station was all wobbles and ambivalence. It was raining heavily as I trudged towards Newnham and a small street enclave, so generic it could have been anywhere. Inside, I was guided to a warm room on the first floor.

'There are blankets and cushions so just take anything you need' I was informed. I said thank you, took nothing and sat in the chair next to the tissues.

'Goodness' I said 'It feels strange to be back in this chair. It's been a while' That's as far as I got before my face started to throb and the cracks appeared. I remember worrying that the box of tissues was almost empty. Eek. Then what?

It is never so much the bodily fluids combo that bothers me. You end up feeling like you're practically gargling your words out. But after the initial collapse, I managed to establish some kind of tear/snot control under somewhat compromised circumstances.

There was nothing new in my disclosures today that I had not shared a hundred times before, but it all felt new and so very terrible. Because I hadn't shared it with a stranger before, a stranger whose job it was to simply listen, to hear how brutally crushed I am in a world without Stewart.

'Is there anything you'd like to ask me?' my therapist asked, just before we ended.

No, I thought, *I just need you to sit there and bear witness.*

'No' I said, 'nothing comes to mind'. And that was true. It didn't.

We arranged to meet again in two weeks' time, and I left the warm room and stepped out into rain, coming down even heavier than when I arrived. By the time I reached home, I was soaking, the sky was swirling with greys and dirty white clumps and the streets of Royston were very flooded. Perfect.

So, a lot has happened since the last entry and I haven't even touched upon the deterioration in my health, re: back, shoulder and neck pain and the irksome, agonising swallowing issue that has become so much worse in recent weeks. Yesterday, I tried to swallow a vitamin pill that lodged in my oesophagus. The panic and restriction in my chest that came about as a result felt how I imagine the onset of a heart attack might feel. I had to induce vomiting because that elephant sized tablet was not going down in a hurry. So, the only way was up.

And all of this gets me thinking about mortality and time. I think about suffering and death and Stewart and how it will be for me when my time comes. *Did it hurt, Stewart? Were you scared?* I pray not.

Last night – a sporadically painful and fitful sleep – I dreamt about something covert and undercover going on in a dark room. It felt all very *film noir* but it was the moment when a man in spectacles, made some comment about overseeing proceedings to ensure nothing untoward happened, that I was shocked awake by the bizarre sensation that something – an animal maybe – had jumped onto my lap. I was trembling and my heart was racing so much that for one moment I thought the occupants of the flat below must have the washing machine on. But no. Just my heart racing fit to burst. And I lay there, and I thought again – *how will it be for me when my time comes?*

Books

Loss gets integrated, not overcome

Megan Devine *It's OK That You're Not OK*

The 25th of October 2017

After a morning of new clients, crisis calls and *Big Bad Trouble* read-thru arrangements, I arrived at my Cambridge practice to the usual slew of parcels. I settled in my room and opened them with no sense of excitement whatsoever. Desperate hope maybe, but no excitement. Package number one opened, I extracted the book. I flicked through it almost as if, as always, I expected something bright and magical to spring from the pages to offer solace. It has not happened so far, but I remain hopeful/deluded.

Suddenly, I felt spiky, sour and somewhat lemon lipped. To my chagrin, there is a section, all neat and compartmentalized, called *The Final Phase of Grief.* Are you having a laugh? I thought to myself, addressing the author. When I chance upon statements that speak of some kind of shift towards *'recovery from grief'*, I smell fear...and a lie.

There is another book that arrives soon, a new text with a title that grabbed me as soon as it popped up as an Amazon recommendation – Megan Devine's *It's OK That You're Not OK.* That's more like it, I think to myself. Don't let me down now, Ms. Devine, I also think in passing. I place the order in a second. *In a second; the time it took my brother to die.*

Next, I set up my consulting room, position the clock, set the tissues and adjust the angle of the chairs. Then, I flick casually through another chapter from today's delivery. I read about 'letting go' and 'getting over' and I groan, knowing there is only one thing I am about to let go of. 'Nothing personal, dear' I say as I let the book tumble heavily into the waste bin.

Scream

Rage creeps up on you unawares

(Mary Stott)

Virginia Ironside *You'll Get Over It: The Rage of Bereavement*

The 29th of October 2017

Tonight, I screamed into a cushion. Then I screamed again. And again.

I'm sure to the average outsider, it may have appeared that I was self-harming, an attempt to smother myself that was doomed to fail. But it was quite the opposite; a wild and weird self-soothing strategy that was neither planned nor expected. It came out of the blue and at first, bearing in mind I was watching it at the time, thought it was simply an utterly disproportionate reaction to *Project Runway*. I'm so embarrassed to write that. True, though.

But it's unlikely that Heidi Klum will ever be the reason I scream into anything, so it must be something else. Something else was hanging around, not with any malice aforethought but simply waiting to be discharged, unleashed, thrown up. So, I screamed and screamed again. That's all.

Halloween

Lately I have been letting my life
Fall into pieces about me.

Marjorie Pizer *Lost in Despair*

The 31st of October 2017

It's quite a walk from the station to that counselling chair in Newnham. About forty minutes all in all, I would say. But the sun shines, there is a chill in the air and fallen, discarded leaves of all colours are abundant and everywhere. Cambridge is quite the picture postcard in the Autumn. Down the Causeway, with the Backs and Kings College reaching up in the distance to my right, I walk and wonder what I'll talk about when the time comes, that time being 11am on a Tuesday morning for the next, well, however long it turns out to be. But while I wonder what I might share, what the focus or feel of my first 'proper' counselling session might be, there is one thing inevitably locked and loaded. I am only making this journey because of the death of my brother.

I ring the bell and wait but for a second before my therapist opens the door. I walk in, shoes are removed. I feel unnervingly relaxed if that isn't too much of an oxymoron. But then I realise; it's not relaxed that I feel but relieved, relieved to be here, in an anonymous space that for fifty minutes is just for me, my grief, Stewart and the whole damn thing.

I sit. The wave comes, slowly at first and then with full force as I call to mind the day my brother was born. It springs from nowhere. I recount the moment much as I did at the celebration of life event. But here it's different. It's not in the same context and it's not a performance. It's intense and vivid and very Technicolour, with bright and shiny Wintery sun that may or may not align with the reality of the day back in '64. Who cares? It's what I remember.

Recalling this and other snapshots of my brother as an infant and toddler, in the wake of his death, is terrible unsurprisingly. I close my eyes and stop talking. Silence. Then, 'Stewart' I say quietly. I say his name again and then a few times more. *Stewart, Stewart, Stewart* as if attempting to conjure him up. Tears roll, mucus flows, sinuses block. The usual. Oh well, so be it. I realise quickly that my therapist's tissues are flimsy and will not be up to the job. But I plough through handfuls of them anyway. There is no hysteria, wailing or seizures. Just the gentle rocking, sobbing, quiet thing.

My therapist barely moves. She is easy to be with. She is a very different therapist than I. She sits, says very little, never intrudes or feels inclined to fill the silence and yet offers herself in other ways. Spiritual ways maybe. But it doesn't need a label. It simply is and it works. It's what I need.

The time moves quickly but I'm feeling ready to go when the moment comes. So, with eyes drooping, I leave slowly, telling my counsellor I will see her next week and silently look forward to yanking a handful of 3-ply Kleenex from my bag *asap* and deep cleaning my nose. I step out into sunshine, blue skies, the quiet.

I wasn't really sure why I was signing up yet again to therapy until today. Was I taking this step because that's what therapists do, a sort of 'doing my duty' thing, I wondered in recent days and weeks? But no. My story is all fresh and ghastly again. In this context, it feels new, revived and unexplored and I'm left asking who exactly am I in the new world order?

Jealous

The only predictable thing about grief is that it's unpredictable

Lynda Cheldelin Fell & Christine Bastone
Grief Diaries: Surviving Loss of a Sibling

The 3rd of November 2017

At the end of a sunny but chilly day in Hertfordshire, I sat with my friend, Eileen, drinking hot chocolate at Costa, laughing, reflecting and looking forward to our upcoming shared day of dance weirdness, *The Strut Summit*, an event originally created for plus sized women to celebrate their bodies through dance. Now, it's open to all the plus shapes, multi-shapes, dance divas and eccentrics you care to mention. Oh hello.

We also talked about family.

'I'm jealous when I hear you talk about Stewart' she told me. I was taken aback. I had never considered this particular 'angle' as it related to my grief and consequently the effect that it might have upon others, who do not feel close to their siblings.

'I'm sorry' I replied but I didn't really know what I was sorry for. Was I sorry she was not close to her sister? Maybe I was sorry that I had been sharing with her all this time, with little thought of the impact. Something in me wanted to somehow make her not jealous so I started talking about the bigger picture of the family, the secrets and lies, the conditional nature of empathy and kindness, the loneliness, the rejection. Then I stopped. Let it be.

Truth is, no matter how complicated, screwy or precarious the tie with family might be, none of us can know how the death of another will influence us until, well, until we know. Any more than I can know – if I'm ever told, that is – how I will react when my estranged brother dies, if it so happens that he pre-deceases me. I recall the conference I had attended some months ago, when a significant figure, both a therapist and acclaimed author in the field of bereavement, talked about the complicated grief that comes to call when a family member dies with whom one had a troubled, ambivalent maybe even abusive relationship. There will be grief. But it won't be the same. It won't be clean, and it won't be easy. Just look at my friend Helen, I think to myself. Her murdered mother was experienced as a 'monster' but I doubt I will ever forget the call she made to me, as she struggled to make sense of the surges of grief that, far from helping her, confused and frightened her way beyond her ability to manage them. When the land of the dead meets the land of the living, all bets are off.

And as for the rest of the week? Well, again, I am reminded of the echoing sadness and gnawing sense of absence. My *Facebook* timeline is punctuated by posts and replies as friends respond to the latest stage production from Impact Theatre, a staging of John Osborne's *Look Back in Anger*, which has been dedicated to Stewart. He was heavily involved with the company, the people in it and its quirky, utterly delightful leader, Pat, a woman slight of stature but a creative and quite unstoppable powerhouse, who crafted the productions with relentless drive. There is a groundswell of deep affection and, in the event that I am not able to travel to the coast to see the play, I am glad that social media offers me at least a modicum of online engagement with all of those performers, musicians, friends and colleagues who miss my brother, currently with something of a heightened sense. Tonight, they gather to see the final performance and recall the person who has made it that little bit more special for them without actually physically even being there. It's a whole world down on the coast that had everything to do with Stewart and absolutely nothing to do with me. And writing that, I too feel jealous.

Floating

We find a place for what we lose. Although we know that after such a loss the acute stage of mourning will subside, we also know that we shall remain inconsolable and will never find a substitute. No matter what may fill the gap, even if it be filled completely, it nevertheless remains something else

Sigmund Freud *to his friend, the existential psychologist, Ludwig Binswanger*

The 13th of November 2017

I'm floating. Whether that be on something or in something, I have no clue. Does it even matter? I don't know. But I'm floating, floating, floating.

Returning to my ramblings and reflections after what seems like an age, I realise now why I had taken such a sojourn. It was all a bit too much. Taking up my pen once more (as it were), something rises to the surface. It stirred earlier actually. I sat with a client and suddenly Stewart stood at my shoulder. For a moment, I was distracted and felt something like a shiver. Then I quietly and quickly snapped back and heard my client's voice again, loud and clear and present. But by then I had already promised myself in my mind that tonight I needed to get tapping the keyboard again and normal service was resumed.

I know when something deep down is trying to attract my attention. This happens a lot. And I get restless, twitchy, angry and start throwing (understatement: it's more like *hurling*) shade. And I float. In and out of time and space and past and present. Grief has taken up permanent residence and like any stranger in your home who has been *in situ* for some time, you adapt, change, accommodate, work around it and then one day, it's a stranger no more. But I'm sick of grief, sick of trying to find the poetry in it, tired of negotiating a new life with it and scared of its tenacious proclivity to pounce unannounced. The farther apart the grief seizures get, the more wary I become.

I still think I swing erratically between belief and disbelief, even seven months on. 'Seven months is nothing' they say. And I wouldn't dispute that. I even say it to others. But even so. As I place my hands upon the glass cloche that protects the ash orb, do I really believe that those little shiny flecks are actually bits of my brother? I talk to it as if they are. But do I really? Maybe I just got coffin ash? When I place that vial around my neck, do I really believe that it contains a lock of hair cut from Stewart's head as he lay in that morgue? Whether I do or not, I wear it all the time regardless.

But along with my wariness, I have a hope. My hope is now that my grief will change. I hope to negotiate a different relationship with it. Currently, I feel stalked by it, knowing that attacks can come from any direction at any time. But maybe in time, it will take its place at my side, calm its ways and we will walk together, having negotiated a new understanding. Only when I feel this, will I know that it has in any way, been tamed.

Tired

The 15th of November 2017

The town seems to give birth to Christmas decorations overnight. Emerging from Cambridge station on a chilly, damp morning, strings of hanging lights spit in my face. I imagine they are meant to look like icicles. They don't. I'm on my way to therapy.

I journey on foot south west of the city as per usual. Unlike the centre of Cambridge, the area of Newnham is pretty generic. In fact, it reminds me of Worcester. But it's not an unpleasant walk and, *Pret* coffee in hand, I stroll slowly to my therapist's house for my weekly session. Actually, I now see this as dedicated time with my brother.

As a therapist, I know how important it is to be dead on time. So, I loiter a while, watching builders across the way discuss where they will be spending Christmas day. None of them sound excited, everything sounds like an obligation. That's comforting today for some reason. And then it's time to ring the bell.

My therapist is exactly what I need at this time; *present*. I remove my shoes, climb the stairs and sit in one of those Ikea chairs which rock because there are no legs as such, just a piece of wood at each side kind of bent into an *S* shape. I hate them. Every bloody therapy room seems to have them. You sit in the chair and then bounce or rock to a standstill, only to find that you're almost looking at the ceiling. But I sit and I keep my opinion of the chair to myself. I just do what I have come here to do. And it starts as always when I close my eyes.

I ground myself. I sit in my silence, eyes closed and take in the sounds around me. Stewart enters the room. My brother is here, along with my therapist who is as comfortable to sit in the silence as I am. She keeps a distance while not actually feeling distant at all. She listens and I feel heard. In the silence.

And I now realise that in these preliminary preparatory moments, I also do my breathing ritual that first became part of this whole frightful journey back at the crematorium that sunny day in May – I gently pat my chest as I softly exhale and it's like I'm exhaling pain, only to breathe it in again on the next intake.

'I think I'm tired of grieving' I say, 'Sick and tired of trying to be dignified, and impressive and a fine example'. I reach for tissues. 'I'm sick of searching for the poetry in it, making it meaningful'. I stop, close my eyes again and I say in a whisper 'Oh my goodness'. *Silence.*

Time stands still in this space. I remember experiencing therapy similarly in the past but there is something else now – an embrace of silence with no wish for, in fact the hope that there will not be, any kind of therapeutic intervention. There is not. I wonder how she knows. Or maybe she's nervous and unsure working with clients who just happen to also be therapists. *Face it*, I thought, *I'd be nervous if I had me as a client.* Or I'm projecting but who really cares other than me? She asks a couple of questions that she described as 'loose ends' from our assessment which relate back to my disclosure about being a self-harming teen and then asks for clarification about my addiction 'breakdowns'. *Bless her*, I think patronizingly, *she's had supervision since we last met.* And I'm probably right because us therapists, we've all been there.

But the greatest transition for me is how my weeks feel somehow different now that I have a therapeutic oasis to call my own. Grief uninterrupted. It is not that anything is better, just that the tapestry has changed. The composition feels altered, transformed even, the picture re-imagined. And all because I now have this time put aside to spend with Stewart and a woman I barely know, in a room in a terraced house, sitting in one of those bloody awful chairs that feel as if they're about to tip you backwards at any given moment. And for now, it feels perfect.

Motion

No one wants to be in pain forever, but if the end of pain means the end of the person in our lives, the pain becomes something of which we can grow possessive

Elizabeth DeVita-Raeburn
The Empty Room: Understanding Sibling Loss

The 19th of November 2017

The times of my life are busy. Following yesterday's *Strut Summit* – it's a summit about strutting and I'm not sure what else I can say about it other than I was the only man amongst ninety women 'strutting my stuff' in heels for two hours on a rainy Winter's day in Highgate – I now need to ready myself for the first, and I dare say last, professional reading of my play *Big Bad Trouble* at London's Umbrella Rooms next Sunday. I would say that Stewart's death has been one of the triggers for this, but I'm questioning whether it's that related or specific. Indirectly, I have no doubt but more to the point, I ultimately think my decision to press ahead with this event is spurred on by thoughts of my own finiteness. *Big Bad Trouble* was conceived, written, re-written and re-shaped over many years as a companion piece to my critically-acclaimed comedy horror play *From Hell She Came!*, staged three times in the 90's with varying degrees of financial success (oh, have I mentioned that it was critically-acclaimed? Just asking).

My brother was an extraordinary force of nature when it came to the performing arts. Unlike myself, this would be modestly realised and firmly grounded in an idea of what was realistically achievable. If he awoke one day, itching to put on a show, write a song, pen a story or draw one of his quirky idiosyncratic pictures, then consider it done. Even if he had to make the set himself from his own possessions, pieces of string, Gorilla glue and sheets of cardboard, he would get on and do it. As for me. Well, if my project wasn't going to play to sell-out crowds at a major venue and require ten set changes, then forget it *aka* the unrealistic/unachievable.

When he died so suddenly, there were sure to be projects and plans that he would never realise, creations he would be unable to complete and stories that would not now be written. It was simply inevitable. Entering that dinky little Bournemouth flat for the first time, an expedition full of angst if ever there was one, the whole environment had a work-in-progress vibe to it – unfinished drawings, the pads full of doodles, lyrics half-written, songs almost composed. And in a flash of something, I feel – *do I? - * I feel – *really? You sure??* - yes, I'm sure - I feel joy. I've had plenty of opportunity, trembling in the company of sadness, to reflect with morosity upon the unfinished nature of things. But here comes the re-frame; so, isn't it better, always better to leave behind a work-in-progress, a life in motion? Doesn't that mean, in a sense, that you never stopped living, creating, forging, writing, drawing, singing? Stewart died in the middle of doing all the stuff he loved to do. I'll have some of that please. So, if there is a bit of inspiration for me in this dark night of the soul, then it is this – to die, knowing that there was always another song to compose, picture to paint and story to tell. Well, that sounds like a joyous thing to me and I'm grabbing it with both hands.

But *Big Bad Trouble* is less a work-in-progress now and more a work-in-limbo, so I gear up, prep and brace myself for a sea-change. Like my brother, I would rather be in a state of perpetual preparation than prevarication, so I take a leaf from my brother's book of life. If this is all just 'wishful thinking' and some delusional coping strategy, then fair enough. But whatever it is and whatever purpose it might serve, when I welcome those thesps to the reading next week and we take our places to give *Big Bad Trouble* its big, bad premier reading, I will be welcoming Stewart, his life and his death to take a seat right next to me when we do.

Reading

If a story is not about the hearer, he [or she] will not listen . . . A great lasting story is about everyone or it will not last. The strange and foreign is not interesting--only the deeply personal and familiar.

John Steinbeck *East of Eden*

The 27th of November 2017

Easy to forget sometimes that for the first half of my life, even more, I wanted to be a performer and that my first employed London gig was actually at *The London Palladium* in the original production of *La Cage Aux Folles*, circa 1986, surely a show queens wildest dream come true. It feels an age ago. It *was* an age ago and writing about it surreal. But that was then, and this is, well, this, the day after the play reading.

Back in London at The Umbrella Rooms, a prestigious and very 'happening' rehearsal space and recording studio in Shaftesbury Avenue, Heather and our mutual friend Sebastian, together with myself, reunited for the reading of *Big Bad Trouble*, or *BBT* as it had come to be named. Four years in the writing, it felt like a 'now or never' moment in the light of afore written 'lightbulb' moment which had cattle-prodded me back in to action. I was guided by an existential reality – do it before you're dead.

So, we did and one day on, what joy! A big, fat, fabulous breath of fresh, living air. I had wobbled and vacillated as the day loomed, scared and unsure, even at times wondering if I should just cancel the damn thing. Maybe it was too soon. Maybe it was too much bother. Ironically, I think it was rather something in my swirling, whirling grief that ultimately pushed me on – I hear it again; *do it before you're dead*. Maybe that sounds a bit bonkers, maybe not. But I think the ultimate driver kicked in as a result of

154

my recent reframe of all things unfinished.

All those bits and bobs about unfinished business were reinforced, from the songs that would never be sung to the half-empty cafetière and the unlaundered clothes. And then came the genesis of the re-frame, which places the awful next to the inspiring, the grief beside the joy. Again, all things.

I remind myself one more time that we're never really done. Because there would always be another this, that and the other waiting for us. We just need to be available and open to receive it (or not dead). There could never be enough colour and there was no such thing as 'finished'.

And so, I did not cancel the reading and instead, for the first time in twenty years, stepped back in to Theatreland, armed with a bunch of scripts and a bag of drag. Even if I dropped dead between Holborn and The Shaftesbury Theatre, the very fact that I was still 'in motion' and passionate and hopeful and armed with not much more than a script and a cheap Finsbury Park wig, will in time bring comfort. Because I would have died knowing that, no matter how cheap, vulgar and trashy it might be, there was always another story to tell.

Finale

I know why we try to keep the dead alive: we try to keep them alive in order to keep them with us

Joan Didion *The Year of Magical Thinking*

The 2nd of December 2017

And there was I thinking I wouldn't have to return for a good few months. How silly of me.

While the dread seeped in the moment I made the decision to return to Bournemouth for the final clearance - no packing up this time, just the final clearance - it was only as I slumped from the train late last night in to freezing, face-slapping air, that I started to feel trepidatious again. What was I scared of? What did I think I'd find? A ghost or spectre maybe, that would rise up and knock me to the ground the moment I opened that door? Stephen, this is not *The Haunting of Hill House* or *The Entity*, I reminded myself. Well, I just didn't know what prompted my heebie-jeebies and it would make no difference even if I did; I still needed to call at the flat before I arrived at my hotel.

I walk into the parking lot at 68 Lansdowne Road and see no lights other than those on the stairwell peeping through the one glass eye of the door to the far right of the building. It is quiet. I jiggle the key gently, knowing that the cranky mechanism can be unreliable. The gentle jiggle works. Then the smell hits me, not damp so much as musty and I'm a little choked by the stench of sweet and sickly air freshener blocks and sprays. Just plain musty would be better. Still, it's silent as the grave.

I am also struck by the warmth, but it feels a bit stifling. Seconds later, I unlock the flat door and it's like the first time I walked in the weekend after Stewart died. Despite the cleaning and clearing and the packing, the odour remains the same. It's not damp but *olde worlde*, not dank but rather nostalgic – a smell that will for all time remind me of my brother both alive and dead.

And I stand there and there's nothing. No ghosts, no demons, no monsters. Nothing. I breathe deeply in and out. In and out. I listen. I sense. I hold my breath. Nothing. Standing there in the darkness, for some utterly perplexing reason, I whisper my brother's name.

Stewart...

Stewart, are you there...?

Nothing.

But I don't feel nothing. I feel at peace and that's a good thing. Then the moment passes and it's over. I flick on the lights and do what I need to do then leave.

And that was last night. Come this morning – and unlike other first mornings in Bournemouth over the past eight months – I wake and take my time. Then, rather than a brisk walk to the flat to attend to business, I make calls, potter for a while and then amble into town for a long, late breakfast. After this, I check in with Jennifer, one of the Stewart cohort and a constant and current companion to me, and little Steve, spend time with Viv at the flat in the chill of the living room and round off the social whirl by meeting with partner Steve. We don't say much.

The last thing I will remove from the flat, and it's practically the last thing in the flat, will be a towel left hanging in the bathroom. It is Stewart's towel and it was there the weekend after he died, and it is still there now. Unlike absolutely everything else, no-one has chosen to remove it, wash it or throw it out. I roll it up and place it in a bag ready for collection with a few other bits and pieces tomorrow.

I will never wash that towel.

Curtains

I realise as I write this that I do not want to finish this account

Joan Didion *The Year of Magical Thinking*

The 3rd of December 2017

We just stand there in Stewart's living room, little Steve and me. We just stand there and while we do not say it, I feel we both time travel back to that Sunday in April when together we walked into this flat, the first visit since my brother died just a matter of days earlier. Then, everything was exactly as he'd left it. Now, it was empty.

'This feels weird' I say.

Steve nods.

'So weird' I reiterate almost to myself and we both wander around the three empty rooms, feeling the nothing-ness of it all.

The last few items are stored away in Steve's car – an antique clock, some board games, plastic storage boxes, that kind of thing – and then there's no more business to finish. There's nothing left, not even a draining rack or waste bin. Again, we just stand in the blank canvas of a space for a moment, acknowledging how Stewart's presence remains writ large even now, represented by way of those splendid blackout curtains adorning every window in the living room, covered in black and red flowers and geometric shapes. It was Stewart in fabric form. Stewart reborn as fabulous drapes. As a final gesture, I take the material in both hands and press my face into one of them, inhaling fully, just as I had with that dressing gown some eight months before. *As it was in the beginning, it is now.* We travel full circle.

But I know when I'm done, I wipe my face and I give myself permission to leave. And then we're gone. The lights are out. The flat sits empty. Stewart has left the building.

Choice

The 19th of December 2017

For the grieving, for those of us who spend our days and nights either slipping silently into awful chasms or lying in the gutter of grief, inert and undone, there will be decisions to make about how our relationship with death and loss will develop, evolve and change. It may feel stuck or there may be a yanking, fear-driven resistance to change, based spuriously on the belief that to feel relief is to forget. But there is always choice. One of those choices might be to not let things change. I get it. I understand. I feel for the terrified clingers, not in some patronising 'poor unfortunate souls' kind of way but because I could opt for this too. But this time, I have chosen something else.

My grief is not going away. My brother is not coming back. He will not be made flesh and we will never be humans together again. And yet I'll do my damnedest to make sure he remains a significant relationship in my life. *Dead but present.*

December has been a doozy as the Yanks might say. It means something outstanding or unique of its kind. And a trip to New York with Viv and little Steve turned out to be just that, the stuff of dreams and magic. But I'm no fool and it occurred to me that while this trip of trips might well be my heartfelt gift of gratitude from me to them, we still only knew one another in the context of death. The bond of bereavement can be a precarious thing. It guarantees nothing permanent beyond the devastation we all felt and that brought us close in the direct aftermath. Trauma bonding is actually a thing, but that bond is not sustainable in and of itself (and who in their right mind would want it to be??)

If we were to become friends in our own right, then we were about to find out.

And find out we did. And we are. What a fucking relief.

Alive with energy, memory, Christmas and of course lashings of glorious Big Apple chaos and bustle that comes as standard, we saw shows, we walked in the snow, we flew high and we sailed the seas (well, the Hudson River anyway). We chowed down on diner breakfasts at Central Cafe @ Grand Central, knocked back bottomless cups of coffee, marvelled at Art Deco wonders and were mesmerized by The Rockettes. The Harbor Lights Cruise was weirdly wonderful and the trip to One World Observatory, the stuff of fantasy and fabulosity. And then, on the last morning, an overcast and chilly Tuesday that threatened rain, I took a walk alone.

If you stand at the south tip of Manhattan, you find yourself at Battery Park and along to the right, an area marked on the map as The Promenade. And this is where I found myself, having walked down from the old World Trade Centre site, just a short stroll away to the north. Due, I should imagine, to the weather, there were few people around; a jogger or two, someone walking their dog and the odd office worker on early lunch or grabbing a Starbucks. And in my bag, I carried a small box half filled with Stewart's residual ashes. I gently took it from the satchel, pulled off the rubber band that held the box lid firmly in place and for a moment wondered if I was about to recreate a black comedy moment where I ended up covered in Stewart, having misjudged the direction of the wind.

But that did not happen.

For a time, I held the box close to me and simply handed over to the familiar judder and shudder that travelled through my body. Then, I pulled the little plastic bag apart and emptied my brother's ash, dust and grit into the wooden container. I closed the lid because I did not want him leaving on the breeze until I was ready. I remember closing my eyes which had obviously been brimming with tears because I recall then how two big hot torrents spilled down by face on either side, almost as if my eyes had popped.

Then I spoke to Stewart, but I don't recall exactly what I said. But I know I told him that I loved him and how much I miss him. And then, as the promenade cleared of pedestrians, I gently removed the lid from the box and positioned myself so as not to get blow back. Then, with lady liberty to my left, New Jersey to my right and the new World Trade Centre towering behind me, I thrust my arm upwards, releasing the contents of the box over the river. 'Fly, my brother' I remember whispering as the remains of his remains appeared in the air, for a moment, almost suspended. Then I watched the larger pieces cascade into the bay while the rest, in the form of a small grey dust cloud, was taken by the wind and flew away inland over Manhattan. And he was gone.

So that was New York with Stewart's old friends, my new friends on an awfully big adventure that rose from the ashes of death. I made a very pointed decision to return here to NYC, the place that had felt so very wrong on my last visit, a trip I had taken just over a week before Stewart died in April. And it's different now, reconfigured almost. It helped us find meaning in the madness of all this, to create something wonderful to lift us, to help us carry the horror of the loss and to be more than the anguish. It takes nothing away from the experience but oh my goodness, it adds so very much.

Birth

I wasn't writing to find peace or resolution or acceptance. I was writing because I had to.

Megan Devine *It's OK That You're Not OK*

The 28th of December 2017

Today is Stewart's 53rd birthday. Unlike Christmas or even the impending New Year, this was an anniversary I approached with a certain amount of dread. It was a bright and extremely chilly day and I had waited up specifically in order that I might make two *Facebook* posts, one on my page, one shared on Stewart's. At 00.02, it was done. I had discovered a series of photographs on a memory stick that were new to me, pictures taken during his 'retreat' to Gaunt's House in Dorset at some point in the early 21st Century where he had taken up temporary residence for mind, body and soul rehabilitation. I added text to the one that struck me the most and as I wrote *'Born this day, 1964'*, there I was again, whirling back at the speed of light, right to the moment my grandmother's phone rang (yes, they used to ring) in 1964, heralding his 'arrival'. Stewart was born. Now he's died.

And to the post, I added a quote from one of the books I had devoured in recent months, this one directly relating to sibling loss; one man's reflections on the death of his brother in his 50's:

There is a loving grief that keeps my brother alive. His removal from my life robbed me of having a full measure of life with him. I think about him almost daily...I want to share life with him. That opportunity on a physical plane was ripped from me. Loving grief keeps him alive
(H.D. Kirkpatrick *Sibling Loss Across the Lifespan)*

And it occurs to me how social media now provides us with a whole new dimension of ritual and ceremony and process. Suddenly, it's not just about trolling, pretend friends and Russian meddling. It can provide a critical portal without which, I would have been unable to spread the word as I had done back in April. Today, I used it as my way of marking a moment. Ironic, that the date of Stewart's birth suddenly becomes more significant to me in his death than ever it had been when he was alive. Neither of us much cared for our birthdays. Until now.

Part 2

This has been a horrible year. I'm just saying it again in case you missed it the first hundred times. But when it came to facing off with this bereavement behemoth, I never really felt alone (some moments for sure but on the whole). Everything though, has its shadow. For me, that came today in the shape, form and appearance of old 'friends' from America and in the context of a trip to the theatre - *Dreamgirls* was the choice, based upon my recommendation. While only A joined me at the theatre, I would be hosting both A and his partner in Hertfordshire for an overnight stay tomorrow. I already felt nervous and I already had misgivings. So, let me elucidate. Having met some fourteen years ago, our relationship had developed over time and, having stayed with each other during vacations and travelled together during that period, I considered them significant and substantial friends. Then my brother died.

I recall how both added their kind thoughts to my *Facebook* post back in April. And then as time went by there was little else. I was touched by an email that told me I was loved. That was good to hear. Then time went by and the trouble was, I didn't *feel* loved. I just couldn't sense it from these two. They were several thousands of miles away but might as well have been on the moon. Then I became aware that any email I sent which inevitably spoke of my struggle and of Stewart was either ignored or the reply never mentioned him. When I was told of the plan to visit just after

Xmas, I responded in the affirmative, stating that this was in fact a marker I approached with dread as it would be my brother's first birthday since he died. No acknowledgement. I was not so much upset as perplexed and somewhat curious. And today the day has arrived and in the words of the Mel Brooks song from the film, *The Twelve Chairs*, I hope for the best and expect the worst.

It was some forty minutes after meeting outside The Savoy Theatre as we settled into our seats, that an acknowledgement came.

'So, was it sudden then?'

For a moment I wondered *'was what sudden?'* as there was no pre-cursor or context.

Then I knew.

'Yes' I offered 'Yes, it was'

I then mentioned Stewart's age and how our father had also died at the same point in his life, give or take a few months.

'Oh God, what did he die of?' A asked, seemingly startled, as if my emails had never mentioned the cause.

'They both died from a heart attack' I replied.

'Oh no. I hate all those genetic implications'

I was rendered mute. Then some moments later came this.

'Where did he work?'

'The Weldmar Hospice in Dorset. He was at work when he died'. I was suddenly aware that I was answering almost with the tone of a person responding to market research. And then, as he clearly recalled that we had a brother.

'Was your brother at the funeral?'

'Yes, we hadn't seen him for over twenty years, but I felt he should know'. I added further detail but there was no response. Oddly, I didn't expect one. And I didn't expect this.

'Was he drunk?' he added after a pause.

Going for the monosyllabic, I said 'No'.

And that was pretty much it. The show, with its recent cast changes, continues to pack them in and the new cast is even better than the originals. As the audience rose to its feet at the curtain call, screaming and clapping its appreciation, I wondered if there were to be other 'final curtains' this evening. I hoped not but it didn't feel promising.

So, we might do well to remember this other 'breed' who I call the 'avoidants'. For all the 'outing' and the telling it how it is from the likes of Megan Devine and Virginia Ironside, when it comes to the crass and intolerable bollocks many speak at us in our grief, let us remember this. There are also the 'avoidants'. That is, the ones who see and sense our pain and our devastation and for reasons only they will ever know, make the mysterious decision to say loudly and clearly, absolutely nothing.

Return

*Feelings of bereavement are bad enough - being stricken with grief,
fear, guilt, rage, helplessness, anxiety and shock. But just at this worst
moment in your life, you find you've got to redefine yourself as well.*

Virginia Ironside *You'll Get Over It: The Rage of Bereavement*

The 2nd of January 2018

New year. Same grief.

C.S. Lewis wrote *'Tonight all the hells of young grief have opened again; the
mad words, the bitter resentment, the fluttering in the stomach, the nightmare
unreality, the wallowed in tears. For in grief, nothing "stays put"…'.* That just
about says it all.

But hang on a minute. There's more. There is the somatic conversion,
the head-underwater feeling, the sensation that is a bit like one thing but
then turns out to be another, the discomfort and the inability to settle
that is something like creatures under your skin or slithering through your
brain. There is the emergence of volatility as if you might weep, roar with
pain or kill yourself (or maybe all three), the heavy breathing of panic as if
grief were earth being piled upon you as you bang on the lid of your own
coffin, in the style of Edgar Allen Poe. Happy fucking New Year.

But truth be told, I have no clue where I am with this. I feel drenched
in discombobulation and I wander about my flat, unsettled and fidgety,
without a real sense of who I am or what I'm doing. But I've had nine
months to prepare for this and I know how to *'move as directed'*. That is, I
do a good impression of being the good soldier, pushing on and through,
fighting the good fight. I have been impressive to everyone but me. As I've
said, I don't care to be impressive anymore.

Every book I have read, every article scanned, picked apart and devoured has, in the moment, offered me something, another morsel to add to the not-so-merry dance of grief and loss and anguish, as if, almost biblically, I would finally transcend. I would rise up and become something splendid. So why am I sitting here, wet-faced with left-over New Year's wine by my side, feeling bloated and old, while torrential rain splats against the windows? This wasn't how it was meant to be. Whatever happened to dignity and honour and magnificence? Again, this is grey. This is flat. This is hell. And yes, Mr Lewis, this is, without any doubt in my mind, the unrelenting return of *the nightmare unreality* of grief.

The orb of ashes is not enough. The pictures, the locket containing the wisp of Stewart's hair, his drawings, the videos of Xmas past, his smiling face, the knowledge that he was happy until the moment his heart became his enemy - none of these things are enough. They do not comfort me because I will not let them. Finally, after play readings, trips to New York, the love and support of friends old and new, the distraction of Christmas and New Year, after all this, something places a hand upon my shoulder and whispers in that familiar brogue 'Remember me?'

And, of course, I do.

Tales

*Sooner or later though, no matter where in the world we live, we must
join the diaspora, venturing beyond our biological family to find our
logical one, the one that actually makes sense for us*

Amistead Maupin *Logical Family: A Memoir*

The 10th of January 2018

Famed gay author, Amistead Maupin has written much about family, his
family particularly, and while he knows how unique this journey is for all
of us, he also speaks of how for many - and I think for LGBTQ+ people
this is so often our truth - in time, we move away from the 'biological'
family as we seek out and create our 'logical family'.

All of this is reinforced by the *Tales of the City* author in the documentary
The Untold Tales of Amistead Maupin which landed last night on Netflix.
Netflix is my new religion. And it was during my indoctrination that I
came upon this delicious new doc. Maybe, I wondered, this could offer the
lift I'm after, considering all things.

So far, this year has felt crappy. The collapse of the flat sale (not to
mention the financial liability I might now have to accept as a result),
my deteriorating digestive issues (swallowing is agony) and a soul-crushing
indifference bordering on depression forms quite the terrible trio and while
I may struggle to settle to anything and little holds my attention for long,
I sat riveted by the Maupin commentary. *Tales of the City* was a zeitgeist-
grabbing novel collection to be sure and for most of us young gay things
at the time, we remember the world it represented and we would swoon
at the very idea of visiting – *deep breath* – San Francisco at some point
and most specifically – *gasp* – Barbary Lane (none us were really ready

to believe Barbary Lane did not actually exist). Having visited since first reading the books, my belief that this city on the bay is truly Shangri-La has not reduced in the slightest, despite a volcanic melt-down there in 2008 when I fled Union Square and, looking like the hottest hot mess, hopped on the next available plane home.

But what most struck me about the documentary, and which fed into my own true-life experience of grief and loss, love and memory was this idea of 'logical family' or, as I had called it at Stewart's memorial service, chosen family. Because we do ultimately get to choose. And, come to think of it, the f-word has undeniably become a more fluid thing in the 21st Century.

So, as I listened to the great storyteller, I was back in a flash inside the chapel circa 9.30am on the 5th of May 2017. I could see myself clear as day, standing at that lectern and gazing down upon row after row of 'family', my brother's clan and community, all now brought together, as loving, despairing family units are, in our grief, out of love and despite our anguish. And let's not forget, I was expecting a handful and no more. I didn't know these people and they did not know me. But families know and sense and feel. Logical families do anyway. I was welcomed in and embraced and vice versa. The judgement, intolerance, shaming, conspiracy of silence and withholding that so often defined my blood family dynamics were now conspicuous by their absence. The estranged brother was here as a representative of the 'old order' but he skulked away from the crowd, a residual reminder just visible in the shadows (literally) and had little clout here. Because everyone else here represented Stewart's very own Barbary Lane.

Speechless

The thing is, grief will absolutely rearrange your relationships

Megan Devine *It's OK That You're Not OK*

The 14th of January 2018

First things first – *how the hell did this happen?* My estranged brother and I stand in the churchyard, that province of eternal sleep, and we look down at the stone, a small but chunky piece of shiny marble, inscribed with our mother's name. It reads *'June Barlow – A place to remember our mum'.* There are no dates of birth or death. If I remember correctly, we three brothers sat around a table in a coffee shop in the nearby town of Droitwich in 1996 and I stated immovably that I did not want dates and so there were no dates. I had influence back then and, while this demand may have had elements of control freakery about it, I just dreaded seeing my mother's death date immortalised in marble for all time. Maybe my siblings felt the same. Or I silenced them. In any event, it was a doomed strategy on my part that helped not a jot. Every visit to the stone was still heart-wrenching.

But that was then, and this is now and it's practically twenty-two years to the day, since three of us stood by a small dug-out at the far-side of Wychbold church and watched in silent sorrow as our mother's ashes were interred. It had been grey and overcast and the air had felt wet and today it feels just the same. I can barely remember what the weather was like a week ago, but I could remember these details from a day in 1996 with considerable clarity.

Today, following a long talk over coffee at Webb's garden centre, just half a mile away, my brother made some idiosyncratically unsettling comment (by my standards anyhow) about visiting the church with me because he wanted to 'imagine mum looking down on us both'. I had only ever known him to be a card-carrying, committed atheist with little truck for anything spiritual so I found this a weird sentiment, coming from him. But I conceded, not as in olden days because my big brother was scary and in charge but because I didn't care enough to put up a fight. *Let's just get this over with* I thought. And over with it was, very quickly. But it was the nature and tone of the talk we had earlier prior to this, that reminded me how disconnected we remained and how it was unlikely that we would ever meet again, come the end of this encounter.

The only reason I had needed to meet him was firstly, to offer him items from Stewart's flat that held no significance for me – some 'three son' photos, a framed sepia picture of our mother as a child in Bo-Peep fancy dress, a passport; that kind of thing – and to present the unenviable worse-case-scenario proposal relating to a joint payment of outstanding debts from Stewart's estate that I felt were a shared responsibility. If he were happy enough to take money out of the estate, I thought, then equally, he should be prepared to put some back. Remember, the flat sale had collapsed, and the bank were hinting at litigation and there were other outstanding payments besides. Well, truth be told, I got precisely nowhere. I didn't hear a yes and I didn't hear a no (which, to be frank, I took as a 'no') and he made sure to inform me that the financial benefits he had so far received were no longer available. In response, all I can afford myself is silence and a resting bitch face as I listen to the deflections. *Note to my late brother: 'For fuck's sake, Stewart, why didn't you write a will? Very pissed off. Thanks for nothing'*

And there we were; two complete strangers sitting together in a garden centre in the Midlands, struggling vainly to make polite, starched conversation before me went separate ways. But there were moments, just fleeting flashes when I sensed he felt challenged by my proposal, where I could have sworn I saw a familiar glint of something in his eyes. *Was that rage*, I wondered? *Wow, never thought I'd see that again.* Or was it just me, triggered in that moment to remember dark encounters and an expression that I had not witnessed in years? It was a look that always foretold just seconds later of a punch or a push headed my way, dripping with red mist and fury. I never won fights with him. He was bigger, stronger, more dexterous. My father had the same look when he was roused. It was positively murderous.

Anyway, when all was said and done, I had heard evermore about his peril-packed, horrible life (as he saw it), how he was a survivor of unkindness and villainy and how he had apparently triumphantly emerged from the trauma of it all. And while I listened patiently, just as I had on the day that Stewart died, I don't recall a single moment in the conversation when he spoke of our brother, how it was for him or of any sense of loss in its many shapes and forms. I sat there either speechless or stunned into silence. I really don't recall which. Probably both. We were indeed strangers.

And as two and a half gruelling hours pass, I wonder if Stewart is in any way bearing witness to this and what it would be like for me if he could. *'I had a very different relationship with Richard before mum died'* I remember him telling me the last weekend we spent together before his death. We discussed whether we would attend his funeral if we ever got word. The estranged one had first come up in conversation when I showed a recent picture of him on Facebook, posted by his daughter. *'Oh my God'* Stewart remarked, shocked *'he looks so old...and gaunt'*. And he still does.

The odd paradox at this time is that after today, while I may have witnessed him walking and talking, my living sibling is 'deader' to me than Stewart will ever be. This is my additional tragedy.

Dreaming

Dreams are another way of helping to integrate the experience of bereavement into our lives. Our subconscious can do sterling work on our behalf.

Virginia Ironside *You'll Get Over It: The Rage of Bereavement*

The 15th of January 2018

This was my dream.

There is the sense of an ending. Maybe it's the end of Summer or a holiday or maybe Summer Camp (even though I've never done Summer Camp). There is a meadow and somehow, I know that many from the group or community have departed. And in this meadow is a stream and banks sloping upwards at the far edges and I say to someone I do not recognise from my waking life 'Wow, I cannot believe so many have gone already, just since Monday'. The stranger nods.

Then there is a pier or jetty and a cabin and I am waking people from their slumbers as they lay all lined up in rows of sleeping bags. And one of those lost in sleep, is Stewart. And in that moment, I think (I don't say), 'Get up. We don't have long left together' and I stroke his head.

No sooner has this scenario played out, than it is night again. In the cabin on the jetty, candles have been lit. I wonder if they pose a fire risk. But it looks beautiful with all the little flames flickering so my fear passes. Now there is a sense of ceremony.

The last thing I remember is moving with intent and some speed to another cabin, this one held aloft on legs and, as I rush to enter, I ask my friend Katherine to join me inside. She is the only person I recognise. Once inside, I collapse, and she holds me. I can barely breathe, and I struggle to speak but what I finally say is 'My brother is about to die again and there is nothing I can do to stop it'. And with that, I am shocked awake and for a moment cannot remember where I am. But wherever I am, I am quite beside myself with upset.

This was not a 'magical thinking' dream. This was not some go-back-in-time-and-change-the-outcome affair. No, this was that hideous Groundhog Day atrocity revisited where I was being asked to relive the unavoidable, the inevitable, the unchangeable. But still, even knowing how I felt on waking, a dream wherein I finally save him with love and fairy dust and a wand or whatever, I think would be even worse.

Throat

But the journey of her life and death was hers alone. As is mine. So I know I am going to die, and I am going to die alone. In the meantime, all I can hope for is to be a loving presence in the lives of those I care about and have such loving presence grace my life.

Maria Piantanida
The Oxidation of Grief: Reflections on Adult Sibling Loss

The 20th of January 2018

During the past nine months, I have had little time or energy to focus or reflect upon my own state of health. But now I do. Realistically, it's more a case of having to. Something is wrong so my focus needs to change.

While as an adult, I have regularly needed a good osteopath or physio for at least thirty years for a whole raft of aches, pains and other muscular-skeletal maladies, my current health issue feels different. If I were to take the leap, I would say it feels serious. I get a sense of something out of kilter that a simple manipulation, pummel or realignment will just not remedy. So, I resign myself to the fact that at some point soon, a camera/tube/device will need to find its way into my very unhappy oesophagus. Because painful, resistant swallowing, weight loss, bloating and nausea point in a certain grim direction, medically speaking, and this activates the proverbial red light. The internet is a double-edged sword in this regard. It is the *Home Doctor* of the digital age. I remember my grandmother owned some dusty old medical text back in the day. It was like reading a horror novel. At the age of twelve, I remember being terrified that I had everything from syphilis to tape worms.

So that voice pipes up, the one that dare not speak its name. That dark passenger that toys with *'what if...'* scenarios. What if, it insinuates, it is something that could, if untreated, become life-threatening? What if it already is? What if, the voice continues, this is the year that you, like your brother, die? I quickly recall, on hearing that Stewart had died, my immediate unspoken reaction along the lines of 'Stewart is dead. Then I don't want to live' which repeated over and over as if on a loop. Maybe that same part of me is wondering if I have instigated my very own end of days. Maybe it hopes that this is it. That's quite a thing to write, come to think of it.

So, with all this life versus death stuff changing the panorama yet again and the ground beneath my feet trembling away, I take time away from contemplating my oesophagus and spend part of my day in London with Katherine, late-lunching on the South Bank. There is something very intimate about discussing one's mortality and I quietly and calmly, with no sense of panic or doom, talk to her of my fears in the light of this dysphagic condition. I am oddly calmed by the fact that she takes those fears as a 'given'. I do not plan to tell anyone else other than Jenna and also Roger, who actually needed to know when earlier this week, I had an 'episode' while dining in his company. Running off to the toilet to regurgitate food every five minutes did, I feel, deserve an explanation out of good manners if nothing else.

But the older the relationships, the more likely friends are to have had their own experience of bereavement as well as borne witness to grief and loss in the lives of others. Later this same afternoon on an utterly dreary, rain-lashed Saturday in the capital, I meet up with a long-time cohort, made up of Jenny and Graham. We have known one another since Cambridge days in the '80's when life was a bright and shiny thing; three of us with our sights set upon a glamorous life in the performing arts. It was all we ever talked about. Today, I talk about Stewart, Graham shares with me how shocked he was to hear the news from Jenny which leads unsurprisingly to reflections and remembrances of others we have known who are now ghosts. Graham tells me about the sudden and unexpected death of his mother, Jenny of her parents both dying in speedy succession of each other and I, still in the rawness of this thing allow myself to recall some carefully-selected moments from the past nine months, cautiously teasing out only those that will not reduce me to rubble.

And all the while, we drink coffee and wine at *The National Theatre* – which seems apt – and it doesn't feel gloomy and dark at all. It feels like what friends do. To them, however, I do not mention the dysphagia.

Jolt

Every man must do two things alone; he must do his own believing and
his own dying.

Martin Luther

The 31st of January 2018

So, I'm sitting here in my flat, my gob is somewhat smacked, and I take a moment to consider, reflect, acknowledge and absorb the inference of what just happened. My appointment with the doctor finally brings home the reality of the implications that have been muttering and jabbering away in my ear in recent weeks. I may have cancer. Seeing that, letting those words sink in, is a chilly thing. Cancer. It's not just a word. Cancer. It's the bogeyman, a haunted house, something in the shadows, a monster, the end. Those are just some of the places you go. I've just been to all of them and my appointment was only thirty minutes ago.

And I know, if I know anything, that if my brother were alive, I would be calling him straight away. I would call him unquestionably. Because that's what we did. But I remember as I write that this was not ever thus. On his final visit to stay with me, when Stewart disclosed his encounter with the unstoppable, torrential nose haemorrhage, the two-hour downpour that occurred just months before he died, I berated him for not calling me. He shrugged it off. He didn't call anyone except NHS Direct. They told him to go to A&E. He did, got cauterized, end of story. I wish I could shrug this off. And I wish I could speak with him now and tell him that I'm scared. Because I am scared.

My doctor, not big on the emotional, relational approach, at first listened to me reel off my list of symptoms, which I did in a calm and considered style. I have known many doctors like that. As a result, I fully expected that I would need to suggest a private option, in the wake of the assumed *'Oh it's probably nothing. Let's do some blood tests'* prognosis. What I did not expect was a response which, while also calm and considered, had quickly arrived at the same conclusion as I – that this could be cancer.

And within minutes, all was set in motion. Speedy blood test requests (Addenbrookes, here I come), stool sample bottles (I'm no stranger to those, following a similar scare in 2001) and a request for an urgent endoscopy (been there, done that) had all been signed and sealed if not delivered. So that's that. All I have to do now is sit with it until I know one way or another. But at least I'll know.

So, what's what, I wonder? My brother has been my focus all day, every day for ten months. Now I need to make space for this. But what is this? All it took was ten minutes with a medical professional for another unscheduled freight train to slam into me. As if the entire convoy that had me in its sights from April 6 onwards had not been enough. So, there it is – I won't be coming up for air just yet.

Dawning

The oldest and strongest emotion of mankind is fear; and the oldest and strongest kind of fear is fear of the unknown.

H.P. Lovecraft *Supernatural Horror in Literature & Other Literary Essays*

The 1st of February 2018

So, this is like standing at a fork in the road. Waking at around 3.30am, my thought process went something like this:

Dark. Alone. Quiet. Too quiet. Cancer. What if. Bald. Blood. Stewart. Hospital. Dead. Mother. Mortality. Helen Dunmore . Tinky Winky. Dead. Simon . Love. Loss. End. Reunion. Relax. Panic. Tubes. Stewart. Scream.

Despite this whirling dervish of a mind, I managed to sleep again until I rose at seven. I spun the previous day's appointment with the doctor over and over in my mangled mind and I know what he was thinking. It was pretty much, I imagine, what I had been tossing around in my head for a few weeks now. So, first stop, blood tests.

Grateful and relieved that I had no scheduled clients until later that day, I travelled to Addenbrooke's in Cambridge hoping to miss the drop-in blood rush (see what I did there?) and indeed, I did – but only by a matter of minutes. I stepped from the bus into startling sunshine and a blue sky and it occurred to me in a nanosecond that this was a day not unlike the 6th of April 2017, a date filled with splendid weather and terrible news. That was a Thursday too. And then another dawning. This was the first time I had been inside a hospital since then, though surprisingly that realisation filled me with little dread and barely a chill. This was, I thought, odd. But odd or not, today I was preoccupied, ruminating on my own mortality, my own emerging sense of existential angst.

I can only have waited in the blood drop-in for about ten minutes but during that time I must have played through the memory tape of the visit to my brother in the chapel of rest at least three times. This environment was packed with triggers, so I was hardly shocked when they all started flicking and clicking like little time switches. So, I close my eyes briefly and linger in the memory, allowing myself to stand next to Stewart, neither of us moving. He is dead and I am frozen in grief. I am screaming inside. He is not. Suddenly someone presses a buzzer and the memory cuts out.

'Number 39?' someone announces. That's me. It's only just turned 9.30 in the morning, but the room is now full so I'm glad I arrived when I did. Ten minutes later, I'm done, dusted, swabbed and gagging for coffee.

So here it is - the fork in the road. 'I'm so full up with stuff' I shared with Katherine last night 'I just don't think I can fit anything else in'.

'And yet you do. And you have' she croaks (she's not normally a croaker but she is nursing laryngitis). And I guess she's right.

Before I left the apartment this morning, I placed my hands on the cloche dome that covers my ashes-to-glass memorial orb and I peered into the precious ash bubbles.

'Well, Stewart, here we go' I whispered. And with that, I grabbed my blood forms, briefcase and gloves and pressed on into the day. The landscape just changed. This bit of the terrain is suddenly rendered new, unpredictable and frightening in a whole new way.

Respite

It is indeed impossible to imagine our own death.

Sigmund Freud

The 4th of February 2018

Having spent four days shaking my fists at the universe, I stop and step back. While not a particularly rock-steady position, it does at least give me time to breathe. My fantasy was that having considered cancer as at least one possible outcome, I was now sentenced to a term of fear, panic and distraction that would make most things, including my work, utterly impossible. But so far, that is not the case. *So far.*

I do, though, find myself seeking an audience with my brother a lot of the time and every now and then, I tend to remind myself that the call I would have immediately made under any other circumstances – those being, Stewart is still alive and able to answer – is not an option. I have rarely felt lonely during this past ten months, but I do today.

So, I wait. But not too long because no sooner has the blood been sucked out of my vein, I get a letter just two days later to attend a CT scan appointment next Thursday just eight days after the initial appointment with my very dissociated doctor. He may appear devoid of emotion and rubbish with eye contact, but he clearly excels when it comes to the paperwork.

Next weekend, a performance to honour Stewart is taking place at the *Shelley Theatre* (as in, Mary Shelley. Yes, *the* Mary Shelley) and I have been invited to attend. But it all feels a bit of a different beast now. Because I would be attending carrying this horrible anxiety and I cannot imagine I will be able to leave it behind in Royston. What I hope for in the meantime is no more shocks for as Mary Shelley herself wrote in *Frankenstein*, '*Nothing is so painful to the human mind as a great and sudden change*'. Nothing.

Contemplation

…loss and bereavement can cause a rip in the fabric of our assumed world, through which unwelcome existential realities may be glimpsed

Greg Madison *Existential Perspectives on Human Issues*

The 7th of February 2018

Unable to concentrate on or commit to the most undemanding of Netflix offerings, I decide to write something, anything. Anything that will occupy my thoughts and feelings for a while. Bizarre NHS anomalies aside, the speedy journey to fast-track treatment has taken me by surprise. In less than a week, letter after form after confirmation fell through the letterbox, bringing me to this moment, the night before my tests, nowadays referred to by myself as 'the big reveal'. And while it is too early to jump on the cancer bandwagon for sure, so much of the paperwork has it writ large all over the place that that's exactly where I am, like it's a foregone conclusion.

By this time tomorrow, I will have a better idea and while I would say that, if it were to be the case, everything changes, everything changes regardless. I doubt that any one of us would arrive here and ever expect to go back to being as they were before. To consider cancer, which is to consider temporality, mortality, our finiteness and the whole damn thing, is to spend time with death at your side or at least, passing through or returning now and again. This is death as my brother never knew it and that's dawning on me now as I write. To have the time to reflect upon what actually it might be like to move towards life's epilogue, not in the shape and form of a sudden, last breath but actually to feel the slide, the collapse, the surrender, is quite something. It is simply an avoidance – tempting but an avoidance nonetheless – to say, 'Oh I'm sure it's nothing' or 'You'll be fine' or 'They just need to check'. Because conversely, it could be something, it may not be fine, and they may find cancer. Or they may not. Us mere mortals find it excruciating to sit with this not-knowing and when it comes to death, if we are totally honest, who the hell in their right mind would, really want to know.

If I were able to keep company with Stewart right now, in this moment, in the nether world, things would be different.

'Shit' he would say 'first me and now this'. And he would look at me, almost to apologise and I would tell him it is not his fault.

'Sorry' he then says, and I remind him again that I do not blame him and I'm just glad he's here now.

We would sit silently in this 'other place' and mercifully he does not tarnish the moment with any of those aforementioned clichés, but simply lets me be. And I am grateful for that.

'Life can be shit' he opines.

Then I whisper, 'Just watch over me'.

'I will' he reassures me 'I always will'.

And as fantastical as this all might sound, these are the words I will choose to remember in a few hours, when that day arrives.

Inside

I will never forget it, ya know!

Bette Midler

The 12th of February 2018

I had assumed that I would be chomping at the bit to write and record, following the events of last week. Wrong. I could barely string words, thoughts or actions together let alone get anything coherent or at all lucid down on the page. I've been stranded in a land of aimless wandering in the wake of the Addenbrooke's endoscopy experience first thing on Thursday, where a horde of the anxious, haunted and terrified waited, like me, to be penetrated and probed. After a while, it was fairly easy to surmise which end of each patient was going to cop it, depending on whether one was asked to stay dressed on arrival or handed a gown with an open back. Bottom line (pun intended), there isn't a good 'end'. I remained pretty much dressed as I was, but as soon as the procedure began, I really wished I'd been handed a gown.

'Did anyone come with you?' the nurse asked during Phase 1, the questionnaire and form signing part of the production.

'No' I replied 'I'm not going for the sedative option'

She looked surprised, verging on shocked. 'So, you're NOT going for the sedative then?' and by her tone and inflection, she might just as well have said *'Oh my GOD! What are you thinking? Are you mad?!?'*

Too late. I'll have to make do with throat spray.

Entering the scene of the crime, three personnel waited for me, headed by senior nurse Anne W, who has for some reason which is both bizarre and a blessed relief, elected to spend her life inserting tubes into people's orifices in search of answers, solutions and maybe even the meaning of life. I liked her a lot. In fact, I was in awe of these people. First off, the throat spray was applied. I felt for a moment as if I were drowning or might choke on my own saliva. Great start. But throat numb and lying on my side, it was simply a case of total acquiescence. I managed to stay uncharacteristically relaxed when Anne said, 'And swallow' which I did and she said, 'we're in' and I retched and gagged in spectacular fashion. But I stayed relaxed and kind of just let the heaving happen. A man called Isaac kept his hand on my head while the other held one of those mouth vacuum things, sucking out whatever it was that was flowing out of my innards. By the sound of it, it was quite the clean-up operation. Unlike Isaac, I didn't have to look at it. And while there's a chance I might well be kidding myself, I chose to believe that his hand placed gently upon my head was a gesture of comfort rather than restraint.

Now this was the big kahuna so after the oesophagus, that pipe and camera (with a light too can you believe?! No tripod though) had to wend its way through my intestine to the bowel and every time it hit a bend, I thought of John Hurt in *Alien* and immediately wished I hadn't. So, I just lay there groaning like a wounded animal because basically I had stopped caring about keeping up appearances after the first retch. Then I heard Anne again 'Open. Close', words immediately echoed by her colleague in a back and forth collaboration that lasted some minutes. At first, I wondered what was going on but came to realise that this was the biopsy part of the show with tiny pinhead sized samples snipped from every area.

And throughout, I kept my eyes closed and for some reason I have still to fathom, travelled back to the chapel in the crematorium on the 5th of May 2017. And I'm standing at the lectern and I'm still and straight-jacketed in anguish. I see people, forlorn and pale and attentive, waiting and wondering both who I really am and what I will say. Then I'm back on the trolley as the bendy camera contraption hits another bump in the road and I groan. Then every now and then, it is Stewart I see in that memory landscape, no life left in his frail body and plastic tubes hanging from his mouth, pretty much how I might appear now. But mainly, I just spend time with him, which offers something verging on solace amidst all the grunts and groans of this utterly trippy and pretty gruesome medical procedure.

Time is impossible to gauge at moments like these, but it ends up taking about thirty minutes. I get the results straight away and while it's not great, it's not cancer, at least not that they can see for now. Something called Barrett's Oesophagus is mentioned but that will require a 'rescope' in the coming months. But let me just write that again. IT'S NOT CANCER. Esophagitis and a hiatus hernia aside, I am relieved and wobbly as I am led to the door and shown to the exit. The hospital is a vast and awesome assembly of buildings, wards, departments, research and teaching facilities and of course, the occasional coffee shop/retail outlet. To walk the length of this particular block takes ten minutes before I reach *Outpatients* and the great outdoors.

I relaxed and shopped for two hours, floating in a strange place and almost walking into walls. Later, I returned to Addenbrookes for CT scans which, in comparison, seemed like a walk in the park, a doddle and a piece of cake. It also provided me with my quote of the week, courtesy of the CT technician, in the shape of 'When we inject the dye, it'll feel like you're wetting yourself'. After this morning's activities, I didn't really care if I ended up emitting fluids from every orifice but needless to say, I did not actually wet myself.

Slowly but surely and having returned home some hours later, I felt myself return to planet earth. I relaxed, ate soup and learned once again how to exhale. Because frankly, I felt as if I had been holding my breath in some kind of soul-eating, far-out, cosmic holding pattern for the past eight days.

Jump

Meaning is something to be found rather than to be given, discovered rather than invented.

Viktor Frankl *The Will to Meaning*

The 22nd of February 2018

In the days that followed the time of tubes, cameras, retching and scans I found myself moving through a three-stage process that started with a weekend of inertia, followed by a week of shock-waves and concluding with a period of staring at the walls, kind of bug-eyed and frozen. All of this just prior to an appointment with the GP to get further results and medication this coming Saturday.

Then, slowly returning to planet earth, the accelerating realisation that I am speeding towards the first anniversary of my brother's death dawns. All I want to do each time that niggle pokes me is take refuge in a hole. Madly, I fear that a rip in time will see me relive the whole vile nightmare from scratch. Not metaphorically but actually and for real and I will live it all again, from the beginning, blow by blow, shock by shock, jolt by jolt. It is, for all intents and purposes, a terrifying fantasy.

So today, I get the daily reminder of the anniversary, a prompt that comes as regular as clockwork. It's like a little breeze of something passing through my soul. At times, there is an avid determination, something that seeks to inculcate that day with a gesture or activity of such epic meaning and inspiration that I and others are lifted to a new level of understanding and consciousness. Well, that's all very well, I tell myself, but let's crank the expectations down a notch. But I am committed to the task and it all starts with one crazy thought, access to the internet and a Google too far.

You've lost the plot, I say to myself. Are you serious? I ask. I bet you don't do it, says my fear. Maybe you will, says something else. We'll have to see, says the wise voice. Regardless, it all has to start with a plan. And that plan is...

I'm going to jump out of a plane.

Spring

If you suppress grief too much, it can well redouble.

Moliere

The 3rd of March 2018

I cannot recall a time like it, certainly not since childhood maybe, and even then, it is just the idea of something rather than a real memory. With sub-zero temperatures, red warnings that foretell of a *'risk to life'*, fog, wind, colliding storm fronts, blizzards and relentless snowfall, this week the country has all but ground to a halt. For most of us, we cowered from the cold and wind and got on with it all. But we're just not used to it and in vast stretches of our world where these conditions would simply be like a fleck of snow on the collar, we might well be a global laughingstock.

And while all of this *sturm und drang* has provided a welcome distraction, temperatures are now on the rise, the snow barely had time to settle in the town before it had vanished or turned to slush, and I am reminded again. It's been nearly a year. In just over four weeks, it will be the 6th of April, the date twelve months ago when my brother died, along with my old self, the life I knew, the assumptions I had made and the world that was. A lot passed away that day.

Tonight in Hollywood, it's Oscar time and this evening I watched Guillermo Del Toro's multi-nominated *The Shape of Water*. Sweet, moving and utterly gorgeous to look at, if ever a movie had Stewart's name written all over it, it's this. Last year, we watched 2017's big award winner *La La Land* on his final trip to Royston. It was the last film we ever watched together.

I now have many books on grief. I carry one with me always and yet at this stage, I simply cannot bring myself to read another word, sentence or paragraph about death. Stripped of any comfort, all they offer is reminder after reminder after reminder. Maybe it's bereavement burnout. Maybe it's too much grief and I just want to push it away, squash it underfoot, lock it out.

I'm still unsure what I plan to do on that day of days. Regarding the planned plane-jump, I have been brought to my senses by my osteopath, who saw fit to remind me about the newly diagnosed hiatus hernia, the arthritis in my neck and shoulders, the twisted sacroiliac joint and the general fucked-up-ness of my spine in general. He has a point and I'm glad he mentioned it. My inclination towards manic avoidance, especially in the context of my addictions, has often expressed itself as some grand gesture of recklessness, ideas that would not occur to me under any other circumstance. Fortunately, utterly deranged flights of fancy to go solo paragliding off the cliffs around San Francisco, a brief flirtation with bungy jumping and a previous plane plummet (I had even paid for that one!) came to nothing in the past, as I realised that actually, there was no avoiding what I longed to deny. And there is no avoiding this. The 6th of April 2018 will arrive regardless. Soon.

Grey

Grief is shit

All of us, at some point.

The 16th of March 2018

It feels like an age and at the same time, a single, fleeting moment, the sense of a lifetime lived in just twelve months. For now, I'm waiting for a circle to close and as I do, find myself flawed by the flu fairy and sapped of any energy reserve I may have had left (a pretty empty tank no matter how you look at it).

So how am I? I ask myself. *Well,* I say, *I'm treading water, not waving but drowning, going through the motions, moving as directed, walking the grief mile.* Alternating between surges of anger, fatigue and weeping, I also find time to wonder if I'm going crazy but that's probably just flu brain speaking (or I'm going crazy. I'm not ruling that out just yet). My head feels like a swamp and my joints ache, exuding not so much a scream but rather a constant whining and I'm glad, at least, that the Omeprazole for the oesophagitis has kicked in and I no longer feel as if I'm being strangled from the inside out. Happy days.

But healthy, normal, wholly appropriate doses of self-pity aside, it all rock bottoms down to this – I don't know where I've gone. Taking just a few days off this week to recover, I'm in no position to gauge where this unremitting back and forth of weird, reality distorting mood-swings is coming from. But I recall a passage written by Hermann Hesse, recently discovered during my ongoing and forever search for others and anyone who may have recorded in words the distorting nature of all this melancholy madness. He describes how it attacks unannounced, both during the waking and sleeping hours, with little regard for any other state in which the grief stricken might find themselves. Everything, says Hesse, from the mundane to the magnificent, from the routine to the religious, can cause distress and certainly cannot be trusted. It could be thoughts of God or an article of clothing. All things are equally doused in anxiety and disturbance. I remember reading it somewhere but have no clue when it was or where I might have been. And yet it has left its mark for sure. It was not entirely a comforting read and yet I felt comforted. Because he knew. He simply, painfully, hideously knew.

And apart from all that, there's this other thing; I doubt how much use I am and what purpose I serve. I am extremely skilled at going through the motions while shrieking away on the inside and I think I learned this at a young age. But I am congruent about my incongruence and the only person I fail to convince is myself. And I'm stuck with me, so I guess the gig is up. No getting away from that fact. And the fact is, life has yet again, become a thinly sketched affair, a line drawing, a threadbare thing with faded colours, the stuff of sackcloth and beige and days, neither full of sun and blue or storm and drama. Just grey as far as the soul can see. On days like today, I don't even realise when tears run down my face, on and off throughout the morning, afternoon and evening. Only the hypnotic, redeeming power of *Rupaul's Drag Race All Stars: Season 3* offers respite and enough colour, camp and shade to knock you into next week and beyond. So, thank you, Rupaul, for being on the planet. She will never know how much she lifted me up when I was digging myself in to an early grief grave and pulling the dirt in after me.

It has often been mooted that when a sibling dies, it can be as if you lose for all time, a part of yourself. Something is suddenly lopped off, like a giant branch. If that is true, then I am not the tree I once was. I simply cannot get used to the me I am now, because without Stewart, I just don't feel like me anymore. I see bits of me and, at the same time, fail to recognise others. There is a brokenness. For sure, I observe myself as if *through a glass darkly*.

These days, I weep alone. I have not been shamed into this. Grief clichés and the avoidants have not silenced me. I have been wrapped in love as much as I have been screwed up in loss and longing these past twelve months. But all this hullabaloo is for me now, in private, when I sit, when I write or when I cannot sleep and climb the ladder to the attic and spend quiet time with my brother's memory box, where I kneel and I grieve and I remember.

Closer

The 23rd of March 2018

A year ago today, it was the biting cold and bitter wind of a chilly New York that had me running for cover to a safe, warm hotel haven. A simple solution. Comfort accomplished. This year? Not so much.

In contravention of my own 'law', I decided some weeks back that I would not schedule my usual break from work but instead take an extended two-week time-out to coincide with the first-year anniversary of my brother's death. The thought of taking leave only to then come back to the date I was dreading just made me feel sick. So, I moved my intermission by a month. And I am struggling. And tired. And fading fast.

But just two weeks to go. Then it will be a year since an unexpected phone call, a train journey to the coast that went on forever, the moment I became a stranger in a foreign land and the day I 'died'. It was, in so many ways, the death of me. *Stewart, you've been the death of me.*

I have decided to take that journey again. After all the dithering detours of planning this, that and the other, I have opted for the option without any bells and whistles, declarations or performance. It's probably not possible to force these things. I find this out with hindsight, but I could not say when it precisely occurred to me. It arrived softly and in something of a whisper, unlike the shouts of crazy, urging parachute jumps, sponsored

196

zumba-thons and heaven knows what else. And it said *'Go to the place where he died. Do nothing. Just be'*.

So, there it is. No grand proclamation, no rehearsal, no emailing to the mourning masses and no coordination of events. Just me, one year on. And I will stand where my brother last stood, in the last place he knew, doing the job he loved with the friend and colleague that attended to him as he faded away.

I trek on, as the grief-stricken often do, bamboozled by a veritable collision of colours, montages and still images. In the end, no words can come close really but today I came across this quote from American writer Washington Irving and it offered some comfort, although I could not for the life of me, say why.

There is a sacredness in tears. They are not the mark of weakness, but of power. They speak more eloquently than ten thousand tongues. They are the messengers of overwhelming grief, of deep contrition, and of unspeakable love.

Arrival

Love is not changed by Death

Edith Sitwell Eurydice

The 4th of April 2018

Well, here I am and here it is; the week that leads inevitably to Friday the 6th of April, one year on from the day my brother died. Looking back on my journal entry for that day is, to be frank, chilling. I had imagined that this journaling malarkey was actually going to be cathartic, healing, a comfort. And it can be and has been. Who would have thought that the written word and the mere process of stringing words together in some shape and form, no matter how random, scattered or just plain grim it might feel, could sometimes (only sometimes mind you) offer something like liberation albeit fleeting? But as I mulled it over in a recent therapy session, it can also result in the opposite – one day, salvation, the next, incarceration, torture, Armageddon. I found this out the hard way just a few weeks back. It was very late one Friday night and the now familiar act of clattering away on the keys left me not so much purged as feeling utterly asphyxiated.

In the midst of a work week and drowning in clients, I spoke with an old friend from those West End theatre days of yore. His name is John and when we first crossed paths, I was taking over his ensemble role in Andrew Lloyd Webber's *Aspects of Love*, during its original run at the Prince Edward theatre. Since then, we have remained very connected, while seeing one another only rarely. Over this past terrible year however and for whatever reason, we have spoken more often. And this week, I shared one of my brother's songs.

Of late, *Dreamcatcher*, an original composition both written and recorded by my brother and the one I chose to play at his burial memorial, kept attracting my attention and, alongside it, I imagined John singing it. Attaching it to a Facebook message, I sent the track to him. He loved it. Calling me up shortly thereafter, he asked if I had 'the dots' (which sadly I do not). *Not a problem*, he said, he knew someone who could transcribe it. 'It's one of the ways people live on, through their music' he said. Yes, I thought, that is the 'gift' of creativity, the arts, performance etc. and as much like a bumper sticker as that sounds, music never dies. So Stewart's haunting, soulful ballad will never die.

On the flip side, my week has been underpinned by a heady mix of dizzy, swirling, clogged-up, foggy-headedness which has fortunately subsided when I have needed to engage in session but it's always loitering, waiting in the wings most of the time. Its cue always seems to be the ending of a meeting with a client. Other symptoms of this head-fuck of a week include watering eyes, diarrhoea, unpredictable episodes of weeping, nasal drip, weird dreams and a restriction in the throat. I could go on.

Retrospection is par for the course, but those wild winds of remembrance have picked up over recent days and, like many a twister, seem to be sweeping me up in their wake. At times, like my journey to Cambridge today, I was carried along by it and when I dropped back in to the present, I simply could not remember where I was going or whether I was forward or backward facing in my carriage. Fortunately, the bluster passes, otherwise it would be quite the most unnerving thing.

So while I may have pushed it just a little bit too hard in the work department, I have just one more day of it before I journey down to the coast to see, to feel, to sense where and how it all began nearly one year ago, on the 6th of April 2017.

Remember

On every 27th of November it seemed as if events were taking place again, almost as if they were branded on a portion of space which the earth passes through at that period.

(Lawrence Whistler)

Virginia Ironside *You'll Get Over It: The Rage of Bereavement*

The 5th of April 2018

Blue skies. Sun. A chill in the air. A year to the day but not the date. I remember.

While I may have grown to fear this day over the current week, it passed without a hitch. In fact, I was very on my game, supervising, counselling, challenging, reflecting and even making the odd pithy joke or two. Occasionally I lost a train of thought or fudged the point of metaphor or symbol but swerved back on track and rescued the moment. That, or my clients were simply too polite to ask me what the hell I was going on about. Then, at 5.30 as I ended the final session and closed the door, the surge surged. I leant against the wall in my consulting room, felt my face bristle and eyes glow. *Stewart.* And then it passed.

Before leaving the clinic, I make a few calls, respond to texts and then wend my way to the station and London. Time passes, a body memory triggered. Something is trying to speed me on, an anxious tic in my heart and a slither of something in my gut. No, I remind it, that was last year. Calm. Be still. He's gone.

First, Kings Cross, where a year ago, I received a call from a stranger, the elder brother. I shared the news and felt not a glimmer of emotion from him, not unlike that day in 1980 when he called to tell me that our father had been found dead in a car in a wood. Then underground I go to journey to Waterloo.

I surface and it's heaving. Bodies flitting, weaving, ducking and diving from up, down, side to side. It's too much for me. I have made this journey at this hour many times over the year. Suddenly, my ruck sack feels very heavy, so I wriggle out of it, but it fails to lighten the load. I stand in the middle of the concourse, staring at the bright, shiny timetable, barely able to read the words and probably looking vacant or on the verge of collapse. So, I just stare, and a familiar exhaustion engulfs me. Bodies continue to sweep in front and behind me. The jumble of words and sounds coming and going, loud then soft as something inside tries to hurry me along again. *You have to get there. You have to get there now. Your brother needs you.* It wants to panic me like it's 2017. But I know better. So I stand, conserve energy and wait for the platform number to appear. When it does – Platform 15 – there is the customary rush of travellers for the gates. I wait and then slowly make my way to the end of the concourse. Because why rush? This isn't 2017.

Circle

The first anniversary is, for many of you, the last significant ordeal of the period of bereavement, and you dread it.

Agnes Whitaker *All in The End Is Harvest*

The 6th of April 2018

This day. Full circle. Return.

This time – 9.15 – a year ago, it was, as the cliché goes, just like any other day. Then all of that changed. Just like that.

Today, rising early, I showered and dressed and then, as I left my room at *The Cumberland Hotel*, caught out of the corner of my eye, just one other person in the long 3rd floor hallway. At first, I thought it was a maintenance person or cleaner, if the boiler suit was anything to go by. But no, it was a paramedic with a large bag in one hand and a box or case in the other. For a moment, I felt the urge to ask if the 'patient' was alright. But there was no air of crisis or urgency to him – he had time to wait for the lift during the breakfast rush, for heaven's sake – so I said nothing. Then I looked again. A defibrillator. Yes, it really was a defibrillator, that thing that jump starts the human heart following heart attack. Like the one they will have used on Stewart a year ago today. To no avail.

Rather than upsetting, this all just felt a bit creepy and out-there, almost verging on *American Horror Story* territory. And then I thought, *if that lift door opens and I see a couple of nuns with no faces, I'm definitely taking the stairs.* Some minutes later, no lift and no nuns so I took the stairs anyway and made my way to the restaurant.

Breakfast comprised of smoked salmon, scrambled eggs, coffee and tears. Again, it was one of those moments when I don't recall any specific conscious memory or trigger, but the unconscious is a law unto itself and these things happen. Unlike with a shaving cut, where you can dab on a blob of Vaseline to stop the flow, tear ducts cannot be similarly stymied. So, tears it is then and I simply ate and mopped up in equal measure.

As the minutes pass, I think about my impending journey to Dorchester, and Stewart's friend, Jennifer, has kindly offered to drive me to the hospice. Every now and then, I check my phone, as Facebook messages and texts pop up. Even an icon or emoji has the power to comfort and warm on this awful day. Facebook may provide a devil's playground for hackers, psychos and fake news but today it's also keeping me sane.

Part 2: The Hospice

We journey to Dorchester in bright sunshine with not a cloud in sight. We talk, laugh, share memories, talk about Stewart. Then, as if in a matter of minutes, Jennifer tells me we will soon arrive at the hospice. I look around. Will I recognise anything, I wonder? I was only in the local area twice, but I then see the hospital and I recognize and remember everything very, very vividly indeed. I walked that driveway to my brother on the 7th of April, I recall. I am tremulous and feel a bit sick. But then, we have driven on and I don't know this next part of town. *So, I'm actually doing this then*, I think to myself. I have no way of knowing what I've let myself in for. Maybe it's best not to know. Maybe I should have jumped out of that plane.

It is just past an expanse of gardening and vegetable plots to our left that we turn right into the car park, a small gravelled area in front of the main hospice building that looks nothing as I imagined. A far from imposing frontage, this looks more like a quaint, old village school building than a hospice. Where do they put everyone, I wondered, because to me it looked so compact from this angle? I stand looking around and let it sink in. Stewart was here. Jennifer and I walk inside and then the building opens up like the Tardis into a space full of warm wood and silence. I hesitate for a second but rein in the rumblings of something that could be too much at any minute. Then, without a sound, two women appear, slowly walking towards us. Jennifer clearly knows them, and I know this must be Caroline and Liz, who have made this visit possible. I simply do not know how to do this so for some odd reason, I shake hands with Caroline but warmly embrace Liz. And then it begins.

With the contact, I feel a buckle in my knees and a slump in my legs. In that same moment, I cannot breathe or rather I lose control of my breathing and it frightens me. I'm gasping and on the verge of hyperventilating and almost as if they were forewarned, I am gently and with no fuss at all, led calmly to an office space that I am told has been put aside for the day. I sit and my body reorients and while still emotional, I no longer feel as if my last breath is on the way.

Jennifer sits to my left as Caroline takes the seat adjacent and when drinks have been provided (I ask for some black tea), we begin. I am now at the mercy of this thing writhing around on the inside and while it may prove unpredictable, I know that both Jennifer and Caroline know that in reality I'm also fine. I am drowning in this and I am fine too so no need to panic. And no one does.

After a few minutes, just enough time to regulate my breathing, Caroline asks in the same hushed, mindful tone with which I have quickly become accustomed 'Would you like to know what happened that day?'. There is a momentary tightening of something somewhere in me and then it's not tight at all and I say 'Yes. Yes, I would'. And I know that Jennifer will now also hear about the events of the day for the first time as well. What we hear is extraordinary.

Part 3: The Day My Brother Died

On the morning of the 6th of April 2017, my brother Stewart arrived at Hammick House in Dorchester to facilitate a training with his colleague Jo. In good humour and neatly turned out in black trousers and burgundy shirt, he parked and entered the building through the back door. It was closer to the training suite and easier than walking around to the front and through reception. If he had, he would have walked past the defibrillator in the main stairwell, that was soon to be used for the first time. In about two hours, it would be used on him.

In fine spirit, Stewart spent some time with Hilary, the manager of HR and, while I do not know the context, comically bemoaned how neither were spring chickens anymore, a point punctuated with my brother's clucking noises and laughter from them both. Hilary's enduring memory of my brother is his laughter as he left her office to begin his training.

At some point and later that morning, Stewart felt an intense discomfort in his solar plexus. He assumed this was chronic indigestion and when it did not pass, he excused himself from the training and made his way to the office next door where he found Caroline. She encouraged him to sit and remained with him while he tried to alleviate his discomfort with antacid tablets. It did not pass. He began belching and at one point needed to loosen the belt on his trousers because it had become uncomfortable and was digging in. Caroline, attending to him for the whole of this time, then informed Stewart that she was calling an ambulance, just to be on the safe side. He did not at any point, I am told, complain of chest pain or tightening. He did not disclose shooting pains in the neck or down the arm. He was not gasping for air or complaining that he had trouble breathing. But she was concerned enough to make that call. Maybe it was her own 'anticipation', a nurse's intuition or something else. But call she did.

Despite being asked if he would like someone contacted, Stewart declined the offer, saying he would call from the hospital. I will never know who that might have been. He did however accept the offer of some tea, which Caroline had suggested. He sipped his drink, the discomfort did not abate and together they waited. Then, as he experienced a profound shift, he said 'Caroline, I think I'm going to faint' and with that she moved to support him. 'Let's get you lying down' she suggested and held my brother as he was gently and carefully lowered to the ground. By the time Caroline had him resting horizontally on the office floor, he was dead.

And completely oblivious some one hundred and seventy miles away, as I concluded my first therapy session of the day, I was about to receive a call.

Part 4: Everything Changes

And in that moment, as Caroline completes the narrative, my bloody fantasy just melts away. This may not have been the story I expected but it was certainly the one I was desperate to hear; that if this was to happen and it did happen, then rather than a hideous, torturous scenario of Stewart collapsing in agony alone in a windowless room, gripping his chest and slamming in to concrete, he was instead provided with speedy attention, immediate care and comfort. He did not know when he said 'Caroline, I think I'm going to faint' that actually he was about to die, float away. No death throes, no terror, just a quiet, silent exit.

So that is how it happened and somewhere in the darkness and thrashing about, I feel something akin to relief, even a kind of gratitude. At times I could weep and wail and gnash my teeth till they grind down to the gums, but I can now also thank the universe with all my broken heart and soul, that Stewart was afforded such a kind and gentle death. For most of us I suspect, that will not be our experience of the end.

Part 5: Hammick House

Just down the way from the main Weldmar hospice lies the little town of Poundbury, also known as an 'urban extension' or 'experimental town' built in the royal shadow of Prince Charles to an exacting specification. It is here that my brother died.

Arriving at Hammick House, I step out of the car and wait. I feel apprehensive and I feel nauseous. At what point might all this be too much? What is 'too much'? Will I know or am I too out of it at this point? I now know the story but I'm about to see where that story played out. I am about to retrace my brother's final footsteps. This has a symbolic resonance quite beyond any words but suffice to say, it is otherworldly.

Caroline meets us at the door having arrived some minutes earlier and

Jennifer and I enter the main stairwell of the building. I see a blue box attached to the wall as I turn towards the reception area.

'Is that the one you used?' I ask Caroline. It is a defibrillator.

'That's the one' she replies and disappears into the reception. As I follow behind, I approach the unit and touch it gently, almost as if I expect to feel Stewart's energy emanating from its electrical innards. It has, after all, only ever been used once, I'm told. And that was on my brother.

After a brief wait in the reception, Caroline invites Jennifer and I into an office. Clearly unable to fully string the sequence of events together, I wonder why we are in an office. *This isn't what I see in my fantasy,* I think briefly. This is bright, airy and warm. Then I remember; this isn't my fantasy. I look around, let it land, wait for it to sink in and sigh heavily as I realise that I am standing in the last place on earth my brother saw. I feel both devastated and privileged. This grief thing really is like a heart and mind-blowing game of extreme emotional ping-pong. So, I sit. In fact, the three of us sit. Silence. And then Caroline says softly 'Would you like to spend a moment here alone?'. I say 'Yes', and I need to trust I'm saying it for a good and healthy reason. With reverence, Jennifer and Caroline quietly leave.

So, Stewart, I think. *Here I am and here you were.*

I'm alone, sitting on an office chair and looking at the floor to my right, the area that Caroline marked out with a sweep of her arm, when I asked where she lay Stewart down. For me, this is now hallowed ground. I stare at the blue carpet. I wonder if by some miracle of miracles, my brother will appear to me. We have just had Easter after all. Surely, a timely resurrection isn't too much to ask. But no. Just blue carpet. So I sit and weep and rock and breathe erratically (again) just as I have a hundred episodes before. Suddenly, I feel the urge to lie down, to fill in the imagined outline of his body with mine. Would that gesture offer me something new, some divine connection, something fantastical or supernatural even? Well, I'll never know because a voice inside me came through and told me in no uncertain terms that this was the line I should not cross. I am warned that it could well be too much for me to process and I may never want to get up. So, I simply lean forward from my seat and press the palms of my hands in to the floor and cry and cry and cry until my back aches and my chest hurts. Ironically, it was the most solid ground I had felt all day.

After a brief return to the hospice, tea with other friends and colleagues and final goodbyes, it was that time. At 5pm, Jennifer and I said our farewells to Caroline and stepped out into the early evening sun. If traffic permitted, I would be back in time for dinner with Viv and little Steve at 6.30. And oh, what stories about that day I would now have to share, should they care to hear them. I knew very little for sure about this day of days, one year and six hours on from my brother's sudden mortal exit. But I do not doubt for a second that how I had chosen to spend this day was absolutely and unequivocally the right thing to do.

So, in this last wave of events, I become the harbinger, the teller of tales. Over the next two days, I offer to share the chronicle with any of my brother's close friends who wish to hear what really transpired that day. And without exception, they all do. They don't know what it means to them yet any more than I do. But what we all know is that far from being alone, Stewart was in the best hands at the worst moment. As far as we can ever know, he was not fearful, confused or racked with pain. That was left to us, the living. But that is the price we pay for love, human connection, intimacy and authentic relationship and, when all is said and done, would we really, I mean *really*, wish it to be any other way? For me, for sure, that is a price well worth paying.

Credits, Acknowledgments & Special Thanks

Special thanks go out to the following authors/publishers, who granted permission to use material from specific publications free of charge. I am deeply grateful.

Lynda Cheldelin Fell of AlyBlue Media and award-winning author of the Grief Diaries series.

Excerpts from **Grief Diaries: Surviving Loss by Homicide** by Lynda Chendelin Fell, Donna R. Gore & Nicola Belisle, published by AlyBlue Media. Reproduced by permission of AlyBlue Media © 2016

Excerpts from **Grief Diaries: Surviving Loss of a Sibling** by Lynda Cheldelin Fell & Christine Bastone, published by AlyBlue Media. Reproduced by permission of AlyBlue Media © 2015

Everyone at Sounds True Publishing.

Excerpts from **It's OK that you're not OK: Meeting Grief & Loss in a Culture that Doesn't Understand** by Megan Devine, published by Sounds True. Reproduced by permission of Sounds True © 2017

Pat Schweibert & Chuck DeKlyen, co-creators of Tear Soup: A Recipe for Healing After Loss

Excerpts from **Tear Soup: A Recipe for Healing after Loss** by Pat Schweibert & Chuck DeKlyen, published by Grief Watch. Reproduced by permission of the authors © 2006

Alicia Dercole @ Penguin Random House

Excerpts from **The Sky is Everywhere** by Jandy Newton, published by Penguin Random House Reproduced by permission of Penguin Random House © 2015

Further Acknowledgments

Excerpts from *Existential Perspectives on Human Issues* by Emmy van Deurzen (Ed) & Claire Arnold-Baker (Ed), published by Palgrave. Reproduced with permission of the Licensor through PLSclear. © 2005

Excerpts from *The Year of Magical Thinking* by Joan Didion. Reprinted by permission of HarperCollins Publishers Ltd. © 2006

Excerpts from *Sibling Loss Across the Lifespan: Research, Practice & Personal Stories* by Brenda J. Marshall (Editor), Howard R. Winokuer (Editor) published by Taylor & Francis Group LLC (Books) US. Reproduced with permission of the Licensor through PLSclear. © 2016

Excerpt(s) from *Surviving the Death of a Sibling: Living through Grief when an Adult Brother or Sister Dies* by T.J. Wray, Copyright © 2003 by T.J. Wray. Used by permission of Harmony Books, an imprint of Random House, a division of Penguin Random House LLC. All rights reserved.

Excerpt(s) from *The Will to Meaning: The Foundations and Applications of Logotherapy* by Viktor E. Frankl, Copyright © 1969, 1988 by Viktor E. Frankl. Used by permission of New American Library, an imprint of Penguin Publishing Group, a division of Penguin Random House LLC. All rights reserved.

Excerpts from *A Grief Observed* by C.S. Lewis, published by Faber & Faber Limited. Reproduced with permission of Faber & Faber Limited. © 2013

Recommended Reading

General

Virginia Ironside, *You'll Get Over It: The Rage of Bereavement*, Penguin 1997

Harriet Hodgson & Lois E.Krahn, *Smiling Through Your Tears: Anticipating Grief*, BookSurge Publishing 2005

Agnes Whitaker (ed.), *All in The End Is Harvest: An Anthology for those who Grieve*, Darton, Longman & Todd Ltd 1984

T. J.Wray, *Grief Dreams: How They Help Heal Us After the Death of a Loved One*, Jossey-Bass 2005

Roland Barthes, *Mourning Diary*, Notting Hill Editions 2011

Kenneth J.Doka, PhD.(ed.) *Living With Grief After Sudden Loss: Suicide, Homicide, Accident, Heart Attack, Stroke*, Taylor & Francis 2014

Max Porter, *Grief Is the Thing With Feathers*, Faber & Faber 2016

Colin Murray Parkes & Holly G.Prigerson, *Bereavement: Studies of Grief in Adult Life*, Penguin 2010

Elisabeth Kübler-Ross & David Kessler, *On Grief & Grieving: Finding the Meaning of Grief Through the Five Stages of Loss*, Simon & Schuster UK 2014

Joan Didion, *The Year of Magical Thinking*, Harper Perennial 2006

Cory Taylor, *Dying: A Memoir*, Canongate Books 2017

Irvin D.Yalom, *Staring at the Sun: Overcoming the Terror of Death*, Piatkus 2011

C.S.Lewis, *A Grief Observed*, Faber & Faber 2013

Jandy Nelson, *The Sky is Everywhere*, Walker Books 2015

Thomas Attig, *The Heart of Grief*, Oxford University Press 2000

Helen Keller, *We Bereaved*, Forgotten Books 2018

Sibling Loss

Elizabeth DeVita-Raeburn, *The Empty Room: Understanding Sibling Loss*, Scribner 2007

Brenda J.Marshall & Howard R.Winokuer (ed.), *Sibling Loss Across The Lifespan: Research, Practice & Personal Stories*, Routledge 2016

Alan D.Wolfelt, PhD. *Healing the Adult Sibling's Grieving Heart: 100 Practical Ideas After Your Brother or Sister Dies*, Companion Press 2009

P.Gill White, PhD. *Sibling Grief: Healing After the Death of a Sister or Brother*, iUniverse 2008

Maria Piantanida, *The Oxidation of Grief: Reflections on Adult Sibling Loss*, Learning Moments Press 2017

T.J.Wray, *Surviving the Death of a Sibling: Living Through Grief When an Adult Brother or Sister Dies*, Three Rivers Press 2003

Lynda Cheldelin Fell & Christine Bastone, *Grief Diaries: Surviving Loss of a Sibling*, AlyBlue Media 2015

For Counsellors/Mental Health Professionals

Susan Lendrum & Gabrielle Syme, *Gift of Tears: A Practical Approach to Loss and Bereavement in Counselling & Psychotherapy*, Routledge 2004

Colin Murray Parkes, *Love & Loss: The Roots of Grief and its Complications*, Routledge 2008

J.William Worden, *Grief Counselling & Grief Therapy*, Routledge 2009

For Children

Pat Schwiebert & Chuck DeKlyen, *Tear Soup: A Recipe for Healing after Loss*, Grief Watch 2006

Wolf Erlbruch, *Duck, Death & The Tulip*, Gecko Press 2009

Resources

This is a short list, but other options will be available via some of these organizations and they remain very up-to-speed in terms of additional active resources. When compiling a list such as this, the challenge is to keep it current. Great looking websites have a habit of disappearing overnight due to funding or staffing issues so here, I just list the most established which at least provide a starting point. Information correct at time of publication.

The Compassionate Friends:
Supporting Bereaved Parents & Their Families
https://www.tcf.org.uk/
0345 123 2304

Cruse Bereavement Care
https://www.cruse.org.uk/
0808 808 1677

Winston's Wish
www.winstonswish.org/
08088 020 021

Child Bereavement UK
www.childbereavementuk.org/
0800 02 888 40

WAY Widowed & Young
https://www.widowedandyoung.org.uk/

Roadpeace (for road crash victims in the UK)
www.roadpeace.org/
0845 4500 355

Brake (support for road crash victims)
www.brake.org.uk
0808 8000 401

Samaritans
www.samaritans.org/
116 123

Mind: The Mental Health Charity
www.mind.org.uk
0300 123 3393

Printed in Great Britain
by Amazon